For everyone who wants to understand Torah, this bo[...]**y ...to an essential aspect of Judaism, and allows you to interact directly with the sacred texts of the Jewish tradition.**

Guided by Dr. Norman J. Cohen, rabbi and professor of midrash at Hebrew Union College–Jewish Institute of Religion, *The Way Into Torah* helps us explore the origins and development of Torah, why it should be studied, and how to do it.

- **What Torah is.** The texts, and beyond: Not simply the Five Books of Moses, Torah refers to much more than written words.

- **The different approaches to studying Torah.** The many ways Jews have interacted with Torah through the ages and how, by learning to read Torah ourselves, we can connect it to our lives today.

- **The levels of understanding Torah.** How Torah can come alive in different ways, at different times; and how new meanings of Torah are discovered by its readers.

- **Why Torah study is a part of the Jewish experience.** How it allows us to experience God's presence—and why the Rabbis called Torah study more important even than belief in God.

This guide offers an entrance into the world of Torah, and to its meaning for our lives. *The Way Into Torah* shows us why reading Torah is not the same as reading anything else—and enables us to become a part of a chain of Jewish tradition that began millennia ago, and remains unbroken today.

———————

"Encourages the readers to interact personally with the text through their own experience.... Opens up the process of midrash, as well as elucidating methods of interpretation.... Could be the first step back into meaningful and responsive Judaism."
—**Rabbi Sylvia Rothschild**, *Jewish Chronicle (UK)*

"A clearly delineated and persuasive guide to studying the Torah.... Demonstrates the power behind the words and encourages readers to study Torah more profoundly and meaningfully.... Highly recommended."
—*Library Journal*

"Accessible and basic, yet sophisticated and wise."
—*Publishers Weekly*

About *The Way Into...*

The Way Into... is a major series that provides an accessible and highly usable "guided tour" of the Jewish faith and people, its history and beliefs—in total, a basic introduction to Judaism for adults that will enable them to understand and interact with sacred texts.

The Authors

Each book in the series is written by a leading contemporary teacher and thinker. While each of the authors brings his or her own individual style of teaching to the series, every volume's approach is the same: to help you to learn, in a life-affecting way, about important concepts in Judaism.

The Concepts

Each volume in *The Way Into...* Series explores one important concept in Judaism, including its history, its basic vocabulary, and what it means to Judaism and to us. In the Jewish tradition of study, the reader is helped to interact directly with sacred texts.

The topics to be covered in *The Way Into...* Series:

Torah
Jewish Prayer
Encountering God in Judaism
Jewish Mystical Tradition
Tikkun Olam (Repairing the World)
Judaism and the Environment
The Varieties of Jewishness
Covenant and Commandment
Holiness and Chosenness (*Kedushah*)
Time
Zion
Money and Ownership
Women and Men
The Relationship between Jews and Non-Jews

The Way Into
Torah

Rabbi Norman J. Cohen, PhD

דרך למוד דרך למוד דרך למוד
דרך למוד

JEWISH LIGHTS Publishing

The Way Into Torah

2009 Quality Paperback Edition, Second Printing
2004 Quality Paperback Edition, First Printing
© 2000 by Norman J. Cohen

The publisher gratefully acknowledges the contribution of
Rabbi Sheldon Zimmerman to the creation of this series. In his lifelong
work of bringing a greater appreciation of Judaism to all people, he saw
the need for *The Way Into...* and inspired us to act on it.

Library of Congress Cataloging-in-Publication Data

Cohen, Norman J.
The way into Torah / Norman J. Cohen
p. cm. — (The way into—)
Includes index.
ISBN-13: 978-1-68336-448-1 (hc)

1. Talmud Torah (Judaism). 2. Tradition (Judaism).
3. Judaism—Study and teaching (Continuing education).
I. Title. II. Series.

BM71.C64 2000
296.6'8—dc21
00-023563

ISBN-13: 978-1-58023-198-5 (quality pbk.)

Manufactured in the United States of America
Cover design by Glenn Suokko
Text design by Glenn Suokko

Published by Jewish Lights Publishing
www.jewishlights.com

Other Jewish Lights Books by
Rabbi Norman J. Cohen, PhD

Hineini in Our Lives: Learning How to Respond to Others through 14 Biblical Texts & Personal Stories

Self, Struggle & Change: Family Conflict Stories in Genesis and Their Healing Insights for Our Lives

Voices from Genesis: Guiding Us through the Stages of Life

Moses and the Journey to Leadership: Timeless Lessons of Effective Management from the Bible and Today's Leaders

1000 B.C.E.	1 C.E.

c. 2700–2200 B.C.E.
Egypt's Old Kingdom; construction of the pyramids

c. 500 B.C.E.–476 C.E. **Roman Republic/Empire**

c. 330 B.C.E.–1453 C.E. **Byzantine Empire**   >

c. 323–30 B.C.E. Greece's Hellenistic Period

• 622 C.E. **Muhammad, founder of Islam, flees to Medina (hegira)**

c. 2000–1700 B.C.E.
Age of the matriarchs and patriarchs

c. 1050–450 B.C.E. **Age of the Prophets**

c. 167 B.C.E.–500 C.E. **Rabbinic Period**

• 167 B.C.E.–70 C.E. **Period of the Pharisees**

• 70–200 C.E. **Period of the Tannaim**

• 200–550 C.E. **Period of the Amoraim**

• 750–1038 C.E. **Period of the Geonim**

c. 146 B.C.E.–400 C.E. **Rule** of Rome

Events

• c. 1250 B.C.E. **Exodus from Egypt and settlement in Land of Israel**

• c. 1007 B.C.E. **Saul, first king of Israel, killed in battle against Philistines**

• c. 1000 B.C.E. **David becomes king of Israel**

• c. 950 B.C.E. **Solomon begins building the Temple**

• c. 925 B.C.E. **Israel divided into Northern Kingdom of Israel and Southern Kingdom of Judah**

• 722 B.C.E. **Northern Kingdom destroyed by Assyria**

• 586 B.C.E. **Southern Kingdom destroyed by Babylonia**

• 538 B.C.E. **Return from Babylonian exile; Jerusalem ("Second") Temple rebuilt**

• c. 500–400 B.C.E. **The Torah, Five Books of Moses, is compiled/edited, according to biblical scholarship**

• c. 250 B.C.E. **"Septuagint" translation of Torah into Greek**

• 167 B.C.E. **Hasmonean (Maccabean) Revolt**

• 70 C.E. **Rome destroys Second Temple**

• c. 200 **The Mishnah compiled/edited by Rabbi Judah ha-Nasi**

• c. 300–600 **The Babylonian and Palestinian Talmuds are compiled/edited**

>   >

- c. 1040–1105 **Rashi, French Bible and Talmud scholar and creator of line-by-line commentary on the Torah**
  - 1178 **Maimonides (1135–1204) completes his code of Jewish law, the** *Mishneh Torah*
    - c. 1295 *The Zohar,* **Kabbalistic work of mystical teaching, composed**
      - 1492 **Jews expelled from Spain**
        - 1565 **Joseph Caro publishes** *Shulchan Arukh,* **the standard code of Jewish law and practice**
          - 1654 **First Jewish settlement in North America at New Amsterdam**
            - 1700–1760 **Israel Baal Shem Tov, founder of Hasidism**
              - 1729–1786 **Moses Mendelssohn, "Father of the Jewish Enlightenment"**
                - 1801–1888 **Samson Raphael Hirsch, founder of "modern Orthodoxy"**
                  - 1836 **Yeshiva University founded**
                    - 1873; 1875 **Reform Judaism in U.S. establishes Union of American Hebrew Congregations and Hebrew Union College**
                      - 1887 **Conservative Judaism's Jewish Theological Seminary founded**
                        - 1897 **Theodor Herzl convenes first Zionist Congress**
                          - 1933–1945 **The Holocaust (Shoah)**
                            - 1935 **Mordecai Kaplan establishes the Jewish Reconstructionist Foundation**
                              - 1948 **Birth of the State of Israel**

To my teacher at
Hebrew Union College–Jewish Institute of Religion,
Dr. Eugene Mihaly,
who not only showed me the way into Torah,
but helped me find my own voice as he
taught me to hear its music.

Contents

   Understanding how the Torah came to be put together, and
   why "Torah" also is used to mean the totality of the Jewish religious tradition. The supreme importance of Torah;
   through it we experience God's presence, re-experience
   revelation at Mount Sinai, and guarantee Jewish survival.
   When we study Torah we discover ourselves.

   The obligation to study Torah. It is never too late to begin. All of us engage the texts of our tradition according
   to our own capacities and experiences. Torah study is a
   lifetime journey and we are located at different places
   along the way.

   The Torah is the product of individuals who lived at many
   different times, yet the Rabbis emphasized Torah's timeless quality. There are two Torah (the Written and Oral).

The Torah contains everything while it is ever-expanding. The Torah is "not in Heaven"; it is the product of human beings struggling to translate it into their lives.

Acknowledgments

O how I love Your Torah! It is my study all day long.
Your commandments make me wiser than all my
Enemies; they always stand by me.
I have gained more insight than all my teachers,
For Your decrees are my study (Psalm 119:97–99).

In *Pirkei Avot* 4:1, Ben Zoma, an early second-century Palestinian teacher, emphasizes that the one who is wise learns from everyone. He buttresses his point by turning the simple, straightforward meaning of the Psalm text—"I have gained *more* insight *than all (mi-kol)* my teachers"—on its head to read, "I have gained insight *from all (mi-kol)* my teachers" by playing on the two different meanings of the preposition in Hebrew: *min.*

My love of Torah—the Pentateuch, the entire Bible, the broad corpus of classic Jewish texts—is indeed the result of having been blessed with passionate, insightful, and patient teachers throughout my life. My deep involvement in Young Judaea, a mainstream Zionist youth movement, in my formative teenage years provided me with my first exposure to vibrant teachers who shared their love of the Jewish people and its culture while touching me with their commitment to the Land of Israel. They taught me how to communicate my own passion to others. Among these early role models, none was more important than Mel Reisfield, teacher, mentor, and lifelong friend, who embodies for me the blessing of being a teacher. It was Mel Reisfield and others whose influence impelled me to study Judaica/Hebraica seriously and to want to share my knowledge and commitment as a Jew with others.

During my years at Columbia University, the Jewish Theological Seminary of America, and the Hebrew University, I gained much from studying with many wonderful teachers and scholars who touched me in their own unique ways. But it was mainly the teachers at the Hebrew Union College–Jewish Institute of Religion, in both New York and Cincinnati, who had the profoundest impact upon me. As a rabbinic student and Ph.D. candidate, I was privileged to study with an array of devoted teachers who engendered within me a profound love for Jewish texts and in no small measure shaped my desire to teach and guide others. I owe so many individuals a tremendous debt of thanks, but chief among them is Dr. Eugene Mihaly, my Ph.D. mentor in our Graduate School in Cincinnati. His love and passion for midrash as the vehicle to bring Torah to life for the modern Jew was infectious, touching me in the deepest way. The breadth of his knowledge and his ability to probe the text from a variety of perspectives challenged me to begin to hone my own skills and broaden my knowledge of our tradition. For me, he was a direct link back to the teachers and scholars of previous generations, and he enabled me to feel the power and the awesomeness of being part of the *Shalshelet ha-Kabbalah,* the unending Chain of Tradition.

Yet, Ben Zoma was correct: we can and do learn from everyone. Indeed, I have learned the most from my students over the past twenty-five years at the College-Institute. They have been my teachers in profound ways, showing me that Torah must address religious and human questions and concerns if it is to be meaningful and relevant. They constantly remind me that the object of studying the text is not merely to understand when, how, and why it came to be but also what it can mean for our lives. *Mi-kol melamdei hiskalti,* I have gained insight from all my teachers, including my students.

I also have learned much from two individuals associated with Jewish Lights Publishing. They, too, have been my teachers. I not only benefited from the knowledge and skills of Elisheva Urbas, who served as the editor of this book, but learned a great deal in the process of our working together. She helped me better understand how to communicate the substance of the text to learners at very different levels while underscoring the message that everyone can learn Torah in a serious way. She is a model teacher in her own right, combining a deep knowledge of the Jewish tradition with the skill to communicate it to others. Much of the final shape of this book is due to her insight and erudition. The founder of Jewish Lights, Stuart Matlins, dear colleague and friend, has encouraged and challenged me over the years to find ways to reach a wide audience of learners with a serious approach to the study of Torah. His own devotion to publishing books that stimulate and inspire people in search of meaning in their lives has been a powerful model for all of us who know Stuart and resonate with his vision.

In sharing *The Way Into Torah* with you and in our study together over the ensuing pages, I share my passion for Torah in the hope that you will find your own way to plumb its depth and richness. May its light ever illuminate your own journey. "Seal the Torah among my disciples" (Isaiah 8:16); "the morning was (and will be) light" (Genesis 44:3). These lines form the inscription on the seal of the Hebrew Union College–Jewish Institute of Religion.

Introduction

My first experience with traditional Torah study came when I was a teenager, in the company of my paternal grandfather. In the eyes of an impressionable youngster, he was a figure larger than life, though he was only about 4 feet 10 inches. Shorty, as we affectionately called him, spent much time with us, as he lived only a few blocks away. One of my distinct memories of my grandfather was that he always tried to get me to return to the synagogue with him on Shabbat for *Minchah* and *Ma'ariv*, the afternoon and the evening services. He would try to tempt me by saying that we would have a chance to eat *Shalosh Seudos,* the traditional third meal of the Sabbath, the *Seudah Shelishit,* which in a pre–cholesterol-conscious era consisted of all kinds of herring,[1] and we would study "medrash." My grandfather referred to midrash, the literature of the rabbinic interpretation of the Bible, in his Ashkenazic pronunciation as *medrash*. But no matter what, it was not something that he easily responded to, since he was a Lithuanian Jew, a Litvak, who viewed the world through very rational eyes. If you asked him how one should define one's Judaism, he would suggest that the person would have to study Talmud and the medieval legal codes. This is what he studied during the week when he spent time in the synagogue. But midrash—this fanciful world of rabbinic interpretation in which the Rabbis claimed that Adam observed the dietary laws, Isaac studied in a yeshiva, and Moses visited Rabbi Akiva's second-century academy—was beyond my grandfather's pale of tolerance and comprehension.

However, there were moments in these Shabbat study sessions, when someone would offer a particularly insightful and engaging interpretation of a passage, that I would gaze upon my grandfather's face and he would appear like Moses descending from Mount Sinai. His face was radiant with a kind of spiritual light that showed the extent to which he had been touched and even transformed by the words of Torah that had been shared. At that moment I knew that I wanted to feel like my grandfather, who clearly had imbibed the power of each word, and it had penetrated the core of his being.

When I think of Shorty and those moments in his intimate Shabbat study group, I think of another grandfather who also transmitted a blessing to his grandchildren, albeit in a different way. Nearing his death, the biblical patriarch Jacob blesses Ephraim and Manasseh, Joseph's Egyptian-born children, with a lengthy blessing, in which he says, "May you spread out like multitudes upon the earth" (Genesis 48:16). The Rabbis deem every element of Torah to be of ultimate import. Every phrase, every word, even each letter is suffused with meaning and holiness, since it is seen as having been transmitted by God to Moses on Mount Sinai. So they pay close attention to the choice of words here. The word *ve-yidgu,* which is usually translated as "may you multiply" or "may you increase," is read literally by the Rabbis to mean "may you multiply like fish," since the Hebrew word *dag* means "fish." As a result, they then draw an analogy between fish and the Jewish people: Jacob's descendants, for whom Ephraim and Manasseh serve as archetypes:[2] Just as fish live in water, but nevertheless go after every drop of rain that falls from the sky as thirstily and voraciously as if they never tasted water in their lives, so, too, Israel, no matter how much they have been exposed to the waters of Torah, the water of life,[3] when they hear a new interpretation of a word of Torah still receive it thirstily and energetically as though they had never heard a Torah teaching in their lives.[4]

This interpretation of Jacob's words of blessing describes my grandfather and his thirst for learning and meaning. We, contemporary Jews, also thirst for meaning, though our attempt to make sense out of our own lives and to better understand our place in life's continuum generally takes on other cultural forms—art, literature, philosophies of all kinds, myths, psychotherapy, and many more. We feel that these forms enable us to express our most basic questions about life and to structure our quest for meaning.[5] Our thirst seemingly is quenched by other waters, and the water of life, Torah, is not even tasted by many of us.[6]

Most of us have not been exposed in an extended way to the study of Torah. We are like the Israelites who, after passing through the Red Sea and starting out on their desert journey toward the Promised Land, traveled for three days in the arid desert and found no water (Exodus 15:22).

One rabbinic interpretation, understanding water as a symbol of Torah,[7] stresses that the Israelites really thirsted for words of Torah, for it was their sole source of salvation. The message conveyed is that no Jew should be without water, that is, the words of Torah, for three days; and therefore the Rabbis instituted the public reading of the Torah, the Five Books of Moses, three times a week: on Shabbat, Monday, and Thursday.[8] The reading of Torah, *Keriat ha-Torah*, in the synagogue, in an annual cycle of weekly readings, each called a *parashah* (pl. *parashiyyot*), is seen as an act of ritual teaching and study.

At most, one who attends synagogue is exposed to a portion of the Torah and to a reading from one of the prophetic books, selected as the *haftarah*, which "completes" the Torah reading for that particular Torah portion. The Rabbis, however, often use the word *Torah* not simply to refer to the Five Books of Moses or even to the whole *Tanakh*, which is the Pentateuch plus the books of the Prophets and Writings, but also to the totality of the Jewish religious tradition.

Even most Jews who attend synagogue regularly on Shabbat have little contact and experience with this vast sea of Jewish knowledge.

Therefore, the texts of our tradition are generally perceived by many Jewish people as antiquated remnants of another time and place, which cannot possibly speak to us and our own life situations. Yet, many of us still feel aimless, rootless, searching for meaning beyond the material. Can we reclaim the texts of our tradition in an authentic and meaningful way for ourselves? Can we be energized and transformed by the words of Torah? Can we find ultimate meaning in Torah, though we will appropriate it in a modern way? How can we find a path back to the texts of old that will enable us to be moored in their values and world-view, yet reach creatively beyond the context of the time and space in which they were created so they can address the concerns of contemporary life?

Today, many people who live predominantly in the secular world would explore the ways that Judaism can relate to the central concerns of their lives, if only someone would help them find ways of accessing the traditional texts, of acquiring the skills to open the texts of our forebears.[9]

By learning how we can immerse ourselves in the Jewish people's sacred stories, whether we view them as divinely given or as the product of inspired human beings, we can gain a sense of our own baffling human dramas from a Jewish perspective. In turn, this can affect how we live our lives and the priorities we adopt.[10]

So let us together dive into this sea known as Torah, realizing that some of us are first learning to float, while others who are further along will be trying to improve their ability to swim. However, recognizing that the act of Torah study is not the same as reading a secular novel or even a beautiful piece of poetry, but rather a sacred task that places us in a chain of tradition that began millennia ago, we should pause to recite the traditional blessings for *talmud Torah,* the study of Torah. The traditional *Shacharit,* or morning service, contains the blessings for the study of Torah almost at the outset of the liturgy. Although many *siddurim* (prayer books) present them as three separate paragraphs, in reality there are only two blessings, the second of which also appears as the introductory blessing before the Torah reading. Since the commandment to study Torah is in effect all day long, these two blessings need not be repeated if one studies again during the day:

> Blessed are You, Adonai, our God, Ruler of the universe, Who has sanctified us with the commandments and has commanded us to engross ourselves in the words of Torah. Adonai, our God, please make the words of Torah sweet in our mouths and in the mouth of Your people, the house of Israel. May we and our offspring and the offspring of Your people, the house of Israel—all of us—know Your name and study Your Torah for its own sake. Blessed are You, Adonai, Who teaches Torah to the people Israel.
>
> Blessed are You, Adonai, our God, Ruler of the universe, Who selected us from all the peoples and gave us the Torah. Blessed are You, Adonai, Giver of the Torah.

These two blessings capture the meaning and grandeur of Torah study in a few words. They emphasize that the study of the words of Torah is a holy act, one that lies at the basis of our covenantal relationship with God. It is the very raison d'etre of the covenant. Torah study is a *mitzvah*, a commandment—in fact, the paramount commandment, since without it one cannot understand what God demands of us, and therefore it must lead to action, both ritually and ethically. It is not enough to study in order to merely gain knowledge; the study of Torah must affect our lives in every way.

We are commanded to be engrossed in the words of Torah, *la'asok be-divrei Torah*. The verb *asak* indeed means to "immerse," "be involved with," and "work at." Our challenge is to be totally involved in God's words; what is demanded of us is to continually be engaged with the words of Torah and to give our whole beings to the process. As we immerse ourselves in Torah in an ongoing manner, it comes alive for us in new and significant ways each time we study. Torah is not static; it is not given (or discovered) once and never to be added to or enhanced. Even though the tradition tells us that God gave the Torah to the Jewish people on Mount Sinai, the second blessing emphasizes not only that God gave us the Torah in the past (*natan lanu et Torato*—God *gave* us Torah), but also that Adonai is the *Giver* of the Torah *(Notain ha-Torah)*. Torah is ever expanding when we add to the interpretive tradition of our people as we ourselves engage with God's words.

Yet, the very prayerful second half of the first blessing, in which we ask that God make the words of Torah sweet for us, underscores what Torah study is all about. It must be uplifting and joyful, something that touches us emotionally as well as intellectually. We hope that Torah study will challenge our minds as it allows our hearts and souls to soar.

It is in that spirit that we begin our study together with words of blessing:

Barukh atah Adonai, Eloheinu, Melekh ha-Olam,
asher kidshanu be'mitzvotav ve-tzivanu
la'asok be'divrei Torah.
Amen.

Blessed are You, Adonai, our God, Ruler of the Universe,
Who has sanctified us with the commandments
And commanded us to engross ourselves in
the words of Torah.
Amen.

1

The Importance of Torah Study

From the earliest times, the study of Torah has been the highest ideal toward which the Jewish people aspired. But when we speak of Torah from a Jewish perspective, what exactly do we mean? Is the word *Torah* synonymous with the word *Bible*?

What Is the Bible?

The term *Bible* comes from the Greek *Biblion,* a translation by Greek-speaking Jews of the term *Ha-Sefarim,* "The Books," which is how Scripture is referred to by the early Rabbis.[1] Another rabbinic term, *Kitvei Ha-Kodesh,* "Holy Writings," emphasizes the written nature of the biblical text, in contrast to the oral form in which the rabbinic tradition was thought to have been originally transmitted. Similarly, the term *Mikra,* "Reading," another rabbinic term for the Bible, underscores both the public reading of Scripture in Jewish liturgy and the fact that this written text could actually be read.[2] The most prevalent term, however, is the acronym *TaNaKh,* which is derived from the initial letters of the three divisions of the Hebrew Bible: Torah, *Nevi'im* (Prophets), and *Ketuvim* (Writings).

The earliest name for the first part of the Bible probably was *Torat Moshe,* the Torah of Moses.[3] Later, perhaps when the five parts of the Torah were transcribed on separate scrolls, it became known in Greek as the "five-volumed [book]," which we know in English as the Pentateuch. In rabbinic literature, the Hebrew equivalent is *Chamisha Chumshei Torah,* literally The Five Fifth-parts of the Torah.[4] The first section is therefore called the *Chumash.* The English names for the five books of the Torah—Genesis, Exodus, Leviticus, Numbers, and Deuteronomy—are based on the titles in the Latin Bible, which were drawn from the Greek translations of the Hebrew names. These names—*B'reishit* (In the Beginning), *Shemot* (Names), *Vayikra* (And [God] called), *Bamidbar* (In the Desert), and *Devarim* (Words or Commandments)—are the first key words mentioned in each book, but they also allude to the content of each one.

The second part of the Bible, called *Nevi'im* (Prophets), was later subdivided into the "Former Prophets" and the "Latter Prophets." The former are narrative-historical works: Joshua, Judges, Samuel, and Kings. The latter are literary creations from the oratory of the Prophets: the many-chaptered books of Isaiah, Jeremiah, and Ezekiel, and the Twelve Minor Prophets (simply an indication of size)—Hosea, Joel, Amos, Obadiah, Jonah, Micah, Nachum, Habbakuk, Zephaniah, Haggai, Zechariah, and Malachi.

The *Ketuvim* (Writings, also called the Hagiographa), the third section, is a potpourri of liturgical poetry (Psalms and Lamentations), love poetry (the Song of Songs), Wisdom Literature (Proverbs, Job, and Ecclesiastes), and historical compilations (Ruth, Ezra, Nehemiah, and Chronicles, as well as the Book of Daniel, which is a combination of history and prophecy).

The tripartite division, *Tanakh,* as you can see, does not involve a categorization by theme, content, or style.[5] Rather, it reflects historical development, representing three stages in the process of the canonization of the Bible as a whole.

As we mentioned, the tradition associates the Torah with Moses, calling it *Torat Moshe,* the Torah of Moses. It is not clear, however, exactly what that means. On the basis of statements such as *"Moshe kibbel Torah mi'Sinai"* (Moses received the Torah on Mount Sinai),[6] some believe that God actually dictated the Torah to Moses. Others believe that Moses wrote the whole of the Torah text except for its ending, the final verses that describe his own death. More modern traditional readers may say that God did not dictate the Torah to Moses but rather that Moses was inspired to write it, since he possessed the divine spirit, *ruach Elohim*. All of these traditional stances, based on a sense of the infallibility of Torah, underscore the importance and power of the words of Torah, since it is somehow perceived as being God-given. Yet, at the same time, modern scholars and readers who approach the text from either a literary or a historical perspective also discover this beauty and power of the Torah. The personal meaning that Torah offers the individual reader can be enhanced by an understanding and appreciation of how it came to be put together by inspired individuals over centuries.

The traditional notion of Moses' authorship of the Torah is based on Deuteronomy 31:9–12 more than any other verses, since it is stated, "And Moses wrote the Torah." Yet, as mentioned above, most readers, even very traditional ones, do not understand this to mean that Moses wrote the entire Pentateuch. Two other biblical passages that help us understand where and when the Bible was written down are 2 Kings 22–23 and 2 Chronicles 34. They tell the story of the finding of the "Book of the Torah" in the year 622 B.C.E., which is recognized as authoritative by both the High Priest and King Josiah. The content of the book is not spelled out, nor is it identified directly as the product of Moses, although it is read publicly and accepted as binding upon the people. Since these biblical passages describe reform measures that can be identified with the Book of Deuteronomy, this "book" probably represents the formalization of Deuteronomy and the beginning of the formation of the Pentateuch.[7] The first report of the public reading of the Torah (as a whole) comes in a ceremony conducted by Ezra in Jerusalem nearly two hundred years later, in the mid-fifth century B.C.E., as reported in Nehemiah, chapters 8–10. It is clear that the Torah had already been canonized by this time, since the writer of Chronicles, dated slightly later, frequently mentions the "Torah of Moses" and knows each of the five books.

The canon of the *Nevi'im* was probably shaped in the Persian period, by the end of the fourth century B.C.E. This would explain why the prophetic books make no use of Greek words and make no mention of the downfall of the Persian Empire and the emergence of Greek hegemony. It is clear also from Zechariah 13:2–5 that prophecy waned around that time, after the return from the Babylonian exile. A tradition found throughout rabbinic literature is that Haggai, Zechariah, and Malachi were the last of the prophets, "the Divine spirit having ceased to be active in Israel with their death."[8]

Many of the works classified as the *Ketuvim* (Writings) were compiled during the prophetic period but were not included among the *Nevi'im,* since they were not seen to be prophetic in nature. Other works, like Daniel and Esther, were simply written after the close of prophecy and were not canonized until later, probably before the destruction of the Second Temple in 70 C.E.

However, there is ample evidence that the collection of the Writings as a whole was not closed until the second century C.E. The fact that at that time the Rabbis debated the status of the Wisdom of Ben Sira, which was not ultimately included in the canon,[9] shows that the collection of *Ketuvim* was still open.

Written Torah and Oral Torah

We have seen that the word *Torah* has two meanings. One is the first part of the Bible, the *Chumash,* which is read in the synagogue on the Sabbaths and holidays. Another is the entirety of the Bible: what was perceived to be the written record of revelation, in many literary forms, as it was grouped over several centuries. It is this larger category—the group that is also called *Mikra* or *Kitvei Ha-Kodesh*—that is also often referred to as the Written Torah, or *Torah she-Bikhtav.*

The word *Torah,* however, is used more broadly to mean not merely the biblical text but rather the whole of the Jewish religious tradition, which is seen as the subject of learning. The commentaries, interpretations, legal writings, and legends that students and teachers have woven around the Written Torah, starting even before the time of its canonization, are known as Oral Torah, *Torah she-Ba'al Peh,* because, as we shall see later,[10] unlike the Bible itself, they were thought to have been transmitted out loud rather than in writing. The Bible—the Written Torah—pervades all of these rabbinic works; the Rabbis presume that their readers also read and love the biblical text, and they refer to it often. But they also go far beyond it. Indeed, Torah in this broadest sense even supersedes the boundaries of these rabbinic books as well and includes the Jewish religious thinking and writing of our own generation. In that sense, to read this very book is not merely to learn about Torah but actually to engage in the study of Torah itself.

The Preciousness of Torah: The Entirety of Jewish Religious Tradition

It is with this broadest definition of Torah in mind that the Rabbis perceived Torah to be more important than belief in God, since if Israel forsakes the Divine, occupying themselves with Torah will cause the light that it contains eventually to lead them back.[11] Thus, the Rabbis even emphasized that the practice of all the laws of Scripture is worth less than the study of Scripture itself.[12]

Indeed, Torah study is more precious a crown—a greater source of honor—than the priesthood or royalty.[13] Maimonides, Rabbi Moshe ben Maimon, the twelfth-century Jewish philosopher and giant of legal scholarship, goes so far as to cite the sages who note, "A person of illegitimate birth who is immersed in Torah study takes precedence over the High Priest if he is ignorant of Torah,[14] for it is said, 'It is more precious than rubies' *(mi-peni'im)* [Proverbs 3:15]."

At first glance, it is not clear why this particular verse is cited as a text that proves the importance of study—as a proof text. How does Proverbs 3:15, which speaks about rubies, prove the point that the Rabbis, and Maimonides, are trying to make? The first step in the answer is to read the verse in its original biblical context, and when we focus on this Proverbs verse we see that its subject is Wisdom, which the Rabbis consistently identify with Torah. That explains why this verse glorifies the study of Torah. But what does it have to do with the priesthood? The answer lies in a rabbinic wordplay.

When we study Torah, we treat every word as a hook upon which meaning can be appended. Here, the difference between the *Ketiv,* the written form of the word, and the *Keri,* the way the word should be read despite its written form, provides the Rabbis with a golden opportunity. The text should actually read *mi-peninim,* since *peninim* means "rubies" or "pearls." Then the passage would clearly mean, "[The Torah] is more precious than rubies." However, the Proverbs text is written defectively, that is, with a letter missing, as *peni'im,* which means "those on the inside." As a result, the Rabbis can use this verse as if it were saying, "It [Wisdom, meaning Torah, and by extension, the person who studies Torah] is more precious than [the High Priest who] enters the inner sanctum of the Temple."

The study of Torah was frequently juxtaposed by the Rabbis to different aspects of Temple worship. Whether they emphasized that when the Temple no longer existed, atonement was possible through an occupation with words of Torah,[15] or that when scholars are immersed in Torah, it is as if they are engaged in the Temple service,[16] an underlying point was that Torah study is an act of religious worship.[17]

Experiencing God's Presence

Since from a Jewish perspective God reveals the divine self through words and can be apprehended through hearing rather than seeing, when the individual is occupied with the words of Torah, the vehicles of divine expression, he or she experiences God's presence.[18] One passage that emphasizes this value is found in *Pirkei Avot*, literally, "the Chapters of the Fathers," which is actually a tractate of the Mishnah, the first code of Jewish law.

The Mishnah, which was most probably compiled at the end of the second or the beginning of the third century C.E., is in the main a collection of the Torah discussions of the Rabbis who lived in the generations just before and just after the destruction of the Temple in Jerusalem in 70 C.E. These Rabbis are known as the *tannaim* (sing. *tanna*), meaning "teachers" or "transmitters." The *tannaim* faced two enormous cultural challenges: the encounter with Hellenism and the cataclysmic trauma of the destruction of the Second Temple and exile from the Land of Israel. In response, they transformed Judaism from a religion based on land and a sacrificial system to one based on learning and prayer. The synagogue and the *bet midrash* (the house of study) took the place of the Temple. The literature of the *tannaim* became the basis for the manner in which future Jews, up to and including our own generation, learn and think about Torah and Judaism.

Of all the tannaitic literature, which includes other legal writing, a growing body of biblical interpretation, and pieces of rabbinic lore, the Mishnah is the most central. In fact, tannaitic material that is not included in the Mishnah is called *baraita*, which means "that which is outside [the corpus of the Mishnah]." The Mishnah was probably the first work of the Oral Torah to be actually written down, and both the Babylonian Talmud and its Palestinian twin are structured as point-by-point commentaries on it. Most of the Mishnah consists of legal material, on topics as wide ranging as agriculture and law courts to the ritual observance of the Sabbath and holidays, which is organized by subject into six divisions.

Avot, by contrast, is the only tractate (or division) of the Mishnah that contains mainly wisdom and the moral teachings of the scholars whose legal opinions make up the remainder of the Mishnah. Because of that, it is a unique source of insight into how the *tannaim* thought about their own experience of learning Torah: as a result, it is a perennially favorite subject of study.

In Tractate *Avot* 3:2, we read:

> Rabbi Hananiah ben Teradion says: "Two who are sitting and words of Torah do not pass between them, this is the company of the insolent, in accordance with the text, 'Happy is the person who has not...joined the company of the insolent; rather, *Torat Adonai* [God's Torah] [should be] his delight and he studies that teaching day and night'" (Psalm 1:1–2).

Yet, it is not enough for the Rabbis and R. Hananiah b. Teradion to urge that we sit and study Torah ostensibly for its own sake, as the citation from Psalm 1 implies. Rather, the act of studying God's words has greater implications and reward. R. Hananiah continues:

> But two who are sitting and words of Torah do pass between them, God's Presence (the *Shechinah*) is with them, in accordance with the text, "In this vein, those who revere Adonai [God] have been talking to one another. Adonai has heard and noted it, and a scroll of remembrance has been written at [God's] behest concerning those who revere Adonai and esteem [God's] name" [Malachi 3:16].

The picture drawn in this proof text is that God is present with those who study Torah, attentively listening to their discussion and ultimately rewarding them. Perhaps the point R. Hananiah makes is even greater. Since the prophet Malachi, in the verse that R. Hananiah uses as his proof text, was speaking in eschatological terms at the end of his prophecy, R. Hananiah may imply, by comparing the "people speaking" in this verse with those who study Torah, that those who study Torah will bring redemption.

One of the most poignant examples of the Rabbis' belief that God's presence in the world depends on the study of Torah is found in *Vayikra Rabbah* 11:7. *Vayikra Rabbah* (in English, Leviticus *Rabbah*) is part of the collection known as *Midrash Rabbah,* which is made up of ten different midrashic compilations, one on each of the five books of the Pentateuch and the "Five Scrolls": the Song of Songs, Ruth, Lamentations, Ecclesiastes, and Esther. These ten independent works were compiled at very different times—most probably between the fifth and thirteenth centuries—and in different locales, and they exhibit a variety of midrashic styles. Unlike the Mishnah, they are not a code, organized by topic. Instead, their material follows the organization of the different biblical books.

Midrash is a literary genre focused upon the explication of the Bible. The term *midrash* comes from the Hebrew root *darash,* which means "to seek, search, or demand" meaning from the biblical text. It is an attempt to find contemporary meaning from the close study of the Bible, and it is a living art form down to our own day with the creation of contemporary midrashim. But the rabbinic period—the time of the *tannaim* and their successors, whom we call the *amoraim*—was a time of great midrashic flowering. Some collections of midrashim focus in the main upon the laws of the Bible, or *halakhah*, and are the result of a close reading of the biblical text. These compilations of *midrash halakhah* cover material that may also be found in the Mishnah, but they start with the biblical text and follow its order, verse by verse, rather than being organized by topic as the Mishnah and other later codes are. *Midrash Rabbah,* by contrast, does not focus upon *halakhah.* It is *midrash aggadah,* compilations of nonlegal material.

Vayikra Rabbah, in particular, is a compilation of sermons on the *parashiyyot* of Leviticus, and scholars assume that it was put into its final form at the end of the fifth to the early sixth century in Palestine, though many of its traditions are surely much older. There, as part of a list of five examples of the idea that the term *va-yehi* ("and it came to pass") implies misfortune, the text cites a biblical verse about the reign of King Ahaz of Judah, who ruled in the eighth century B.C.E.:

> "And it came to pass in the days of Ahaz" [Isaiah 7:1]. What was the misfortune *[tzarah]* that took place at that time? "The Arameans from the east and the Philistines from the west...devoured Israel." The matter [Israel's situation] may be compared to a king who handed over his son to a tutor who hated [the son]. The tutor thought, "If I kill him now, I will be liable for the death penalty before the king. So what I will do is remove his wet nurse and he will die on his own." So thought Ahaz, "If there are no kids, there will be no he-goats. If there are no he-goats, there will be no flock. If there is no flock, there will be no shepherd. If there is no shepherd, there will be no world." So Ahaz planned: "If there are no children, there will be no disciples. If there are no disciples, there will be no sages. If there are no sages, there will be no Torah. If there is no Torah, there will be no synagogues and schools. If there are no synagogues and schools, then the Holy One, Blessed be God, will not allow His Presence to rest in the world." What did he do? He went and locked the synagogues and schools. This comports with the following verse: "Bind up the testimony; seal the Torah among my disciples" [Isaiah 8:16].[19]

What is the primary message for the Rabbis who shaped this tradition, who lived some time after the destruction of the Temple in Jerusalem at the hands of the Romans? The Rabbis attribute to Ahaz actions he could not have performed—the closing of the synagogues and schools *(batei midrashot)*, rabbinic institutions of their own day that didn't exist in his time. In so doing, they confront the issue of why God brought destruction and exile upon them. Note the different historical levels intertwined here: we have a tradition in a late fifth-century compilation *(Vayikra Rabbah)*, which speaks of the actions of an eighth-century B.C.E. king (Ahaz) in order to symbolize the conditions of Jewish life at the end of the first century and beyond. The message is clear: the people of Israel always suffer because of the neglect of Torah study. When the wet nurse is removed, the children will not flourish. What does the wet nurse who provides the child with sustenance symbolize?[20] Clearly, either the Torah itself or the institution in which it is studied and preserved: the *bet midrash* (the school).

In trying to understand the analogies used in this passage, we can uncover several powerful ironies. First, in the opening analogy, the king hands his son over to a tutor, for which the Rabbis use the Greek word *pedagogos*. The Rabbis often used terms, concepts, and symbols from the common culture for their own purposes. In the Greco-Roman culture surrounding the Rabbis at the time of the destruction and beyond, the role of the *pedagogos* is to raise and educate the child, to insure that he grow up with the proper values and knowledge. He is the consummate teacher. Yet, here, the *pedagogos*, who symbolizes Ahaz, seeks to kill the son, the people of Israel. The one entrusted with the life of the child functions in a diametrically opposite manner. Second, Ahaz rationalizes that if there is no flock, there will be no shepherd. If the flock represents the people of Israel, who is the shepherd? Perhaps we have an ironic double entendre. If the shepherd is the king who leads the people, surely Ahaz suffers defeat as a result of his actions.

Though he intends to remove the source of nourishment of the child, in the end, he himself is killed. Yet, in rabbinic literature, the Shepherd usually symbolizes God. And even though God's presence is no longer among them at the end of the passage, God surely still exists.

Third, to make their point, the Rabbis have not hesitated to turn the meaning of the proof text from Isaiah 8 on its head. The straightforward intent of Isaiah's words, "Bind up the testimony; seal the Torah among my disciples," is positive. The prophet, in relaying God's words, urges that Torah be ever part of the lives of God's people and its prophets and leaders. In our passage from *Vayikra Rabbah,* however, it is used to prove that Ahaz, by closing up the *batei midrash* (the schools), bound up the words of Torah and sealed it away, thus preventing the people from accessing it.

In the end, this passage's message rings loud: If there is no Torah study, God's presence will not be encountered in the world. Torah study is the key to the people's relationship with God and to their survival.

In a more extended and florid metaphor, the Jewish mystics of the late Middle Ages went even further, asserting that God's transcendent being Itself is expressed at least in part in Torah; that God's ineffable name is woven into the fabric of Torah, which is a living text.[21] Therefore, not only is the one who seeks after God drawn to Torah, which the mystics describe as God's garmented bride, but he or she can strip away the garments of Torah—its simple, surface meaning—and, plumbing its depth, become one with the Divine:

> The Torah [in this world] is robed in a material garment just as humankind [in its corporeal condition]. But when humans will rise up from their physical/material condition to a more subtle [spiritual] state, so will the material manifestation of the Torah be altered and its spiritual essence will be apprehended in ever higher levels of reality.[22]

Standing in the Line from Sinai

From the point of view of the Rabbis, all that is spiritual began with the moment of revelation at Mount Sinai, with the Torah given to Moses. It will culminate with the text of Torah that the messiah will teach at the time of redemption, in the world to come that they picture as a great yeshiva on high.[23] And when we human beings engage in Torah study, a new link is forged in the Chain of Tradition, the *Shalshelet ha-Kabbalah*, begun at Sinai.

At every moment when a student of Torah discovers new meaning, the original experience of revelation is re-created. In *Midrash Shir ha-Shirim Rabbah*, the volume of *Midrash Rabbah* that covers the Song of Songs, the early second-century teacher Ben Azzai is mentioned in this regard:

> Once when Ben Azzai sat and expounded, the fire danced around him. They went and informed R. Akiva...[who] went to him and said to him: "I hear that as you were expounding, the fire flashed around you.... Were you perhaps delving into the secrets of [Ezekiel's] chariot?" "No," he replied, "I was only linking up the words of the Torah with one another and then with the words of the Prophets, and the Prophets with the Writings. And the words rejoiced as when they were delivered from Sinai, and they were as sweet as their original utterance. Were they not originally given in fire, in accordance with the text, 'And the mountain was burning with fire?'" (Deuteronomy 4:11).[24]

As the contemporary rabbinic scholar Daniel Boyarin points out, Ben Azzai does not claim to have uncovered the original meaning or the inner, deep meaning of Torah, but only to have read Torah midrashically, using one set of verses to interpret another as in the midrashic texts we have read. But by reading Torah in this way he was able to reconstitute the original experience of the revelation at Sinai. The fire that was evident at Sinai, when God conveyed the Torah to Moses, as Exodus 19:18 tells us ("Mount Sinai was all in smoke, for the Lord came down upon it in fire"), is again experienced as Ben Azzai joins verses from the three parts of the Hebrew Bible—Torah, *Nevi'im* (Prophets) and *Ketuvim* (Writings)—as we have noted, together known by the acronym *TaNaKh*. Interpreting texts by means of connecting one text to another, or by revealing the link between texts and the historical context in which they are produced, the student of Torah *re-cites,* according to Boyarin, the word of God,[25] and so re-creates the original moment of revelation.

Note the following passage from the Babylonian Talmud in this regard. The Babylonian Talmud, like its Palestinian counterpart, is structured as a commentary on the text of the Mishnah. It is made up of the teachings of both the *tannaim,* the teachers who lived before the compilation of the Mishnah, many of whose opinions are cited in the Mishnah itself, and those of the *amoraim,* the teachers of the third to fifth centuries. Modern scholars believe that the Babylonian Talmud was completed for the most part by the end of the fifth century. In Tractate *Kiddushin* 30a, the tractate on marriage law, the Rabbis underscore the notion that in the moment when an individual studies Torah it is as if he or she stands in a line that stretches from Sinai to the messianic era:

> Now, is a grandfather under the obligation [to teach his grandson Torah]? Surely it was taught:
> "And you shall teach *(limadetem)* them [the words of Torah] to your sons" [Deuteronomy 11:19], [therefore, the rabbis argue] but not to your sons' sons. But [if this is so], how do I [reconcile this with] the verse: "And you shall make known *(vehodatem)* to your sons, and to your sons' sons" [the words of Torah] (Deuteronomy 4:9) [which states 'sons' sons' explicitly]? It shows that to the one who teaches his

son Torah, Scripture ascribes merit as though he had taught his son and his sons' sons until the end of time...R. Joshua ben Levi said: He who teaches his grandson Torah, Scripture regards him as though he had received it [Torah directly] from Mount Sinai, [because] it is [then] said, "And you shall make known to your sons and your sons' sons," it is followed [immediately] by, "That is the day that you stood before Adonai, your God, at Horeb" [Deuteronomy 4:10].

As we have seen before, in midrashim like this, the Rabbis create meaning that is not found explicitly in the biblical text. Yet, here, again, what makes that new meaning possible is the close attention that the Rabbis pay to every word of that very text. In this passage, there are two hooks upon which the Rabbis can append their message, both involving the relationship between a pair of biblical verses. The first part of the passage turns on the seeming contradiction between Deuteronomy 11:19 and Deuteronomy 4:9, when they are read literally. The first states that one must teach his son Torah, and the Rabbis quoted here assert that sons here means that the obligation applies only to one's son and to no one else—not to one's daughter, for example, but in the case under discussion also not to one's grandson. The second, on the other hand, emphasizes the obligation to make the words of Torah known to one's sons' sons. To reconcile the two, the Rabbis pay attention to the different verbs used in these two verses: "teach *(limadetem)* your sons" and "make known *(hodatem)* to your sons and to your sons' sons." As a result, they can argue that one is obligated only to teach one's sons (since the verb is *lamad,* meaning "teach"); yet, by doing so, one will insure that Torah is alive for all future generations—Torah will be known (the verb here is *hoda',* meaning "make known") to his grandchildren and beyond. Teaching one's children is tantamount to teaching all of one's progeny until the end of time! Every word, phrase, even every letter of Scripture is grist for the interpreter's mill.

In the second half of our passage, the connection between the two verses that provides the basis for the creation of meaning is not a word or phrase but rather their close proximity in the biblical text.[26] R. Joshua b. Levi is said to argue that because the verse of Torah that states "You shall make known to your sons and your sons' sons" is directly followed by "That is the day you stood before God at Horeb,"[27] it means that having taught his progeny Torah, it is as if he himself had experienced Sinai.

The Rabbis even say that when an individual clings to the sages and to their teachings, it is as if he or she ascends to heaven and receives the Torah directly from God.[28] Therefore, according to *Pirkei Avot* 6:3, "He who learns one chapter, or one law, or one verse, or even one letter [of Torah] from another must treat him with the utmost honor." Conversely, one's disciples are considered one's own children, according to the tradition,[29] and that it is as if one had created them![30] The relationship of teacher and student is both an affirmation of God's promise of ultimate redemption and the vehicle for bringing it to fruition. This is poignantly underscored by the fact that in the tradition the names ascribed by students of Torah to the messiah are the very names of their own teachers: Shilo, Yinnon, Haninah, and Menachem.[31] Indeed, the messianic age is associated in the tradition with the study of Torah. Maimonides ends his own encyclopedic fourteen-part codification of Jewish law, the *Mishneh Torah,* with these words:

> The sages...have longed for the days of the Messiah, not in the hope of establishing their rule over the whole earth, nor out of their desire to exercise dominion over the idolaters,...but in order that they may be free to study the Torah and its wisdom without oppression or interference and so gain eternal life.[32]

Torah Study Guarantees Jewish Survival

The Rabbis emphasize that the study of Torah is the only guarantee of the future for the Jewish people. With the loss of political autonomy in the year 70 C.E. and even national territory, Jews became solely dependent upon Torah and its interpretation for their survival.[33] Even in the context of persecution under Rome in the second century, when the study of Torah was outlawed by the Emperor Hadrian, the Rabbis emphasized that Torah was the lifeblood of the Jewish people. One classic example of this appears in the Babylonian Talmud, commenting on Tractate *B'rakhot,* or Blessings, of the Mishnah. This passage, found on page 61b, is one of many about the wisdom and saintliness of Rabbi Akiva, perhaps the most famous of *tannaim,* who taught at the time of the Hadrianic persecutions in the third and fourth decades of the second century, two generations after the destruction of the Second Temple. The story is said to have taken place near the end of his life, after the brutal disappointment of the idealistic but ill-fated Bar Kokhba rebellion. The opening phrase of this passage, *teno rabbanan* (our rabbis taught), signals that this story is a *baraita,* one of the "outside" texts that came down from the *tannaim* but was not included in the Mishnah.

Our rabbis taught: Once the wicked government [of Rome] issued a degree forbidding the Jews to study and observe the Torah. Pappus b. Judah came and found R. Akiva publicly gathering people to study Torah with him. [Pappus] said to him: "Akiva, are you not afraid of the government?" He replied: "I will explain it to you with a parable: A fox was once walking alongside a river, and he saw fish moving in swarms to and fro. He said to them: From what are you fleeing? They replied: From the nets cast for us by men. He said to them: Do you want to come up on the dry land so that you and I can live together [in peace] in the way that my ancestors lived with yours? They replied: You are not clever but foolish. If we are afraid in the element in which we live, how much the more so [should we be afraid] in the element in which we would die! So it is with us. If such is our condition when we sit and study the Torah, of which it is written, 'For that is your life and the length of your days' [Deuteronomy 30:20], if we go and neglect it, how much worse off will we be?"

This simple story and its parable illustrate the ultimate importance of the study of Torah. Parables, or *meshalim*, appear frequently in midrash and in aggadic, nonlegal, parts of the Talmud.[34] This parable is well known in other cultures and is even one of Aesop's fables. But in this rendition, the fish represent the Jewish people, who—as we saw elsewhere—live in water, symbolizing the Torah, the water of life *(mayim chayim)*, and who fear being removed from the source of their existence. The Romans (the fishermen) attempt to trap the fish in their nets (the laws they have promulgated) and the fox (in this case, Pappus b. Judah, who seems to be portrayed as a kind of assimilationist who wants his fellow Jews to live in peace with the Roman power) counsels them to come onto the dry land in order to escape their predators. On the surface, his counsel seems reasonable: if they abandon the Torah, they will escape Roman persecution. Little does he know, however, that abandoning the Torah will not guarantee survival (in the continuation of the passage, Pappus, like Akiva, is arrested and killed by the Romans), and that in the process of doing so, the one who leaves the water behind will also lose the promise of ultimate salvation. Akiva uses the parable to build an argument from a minor premise ("If we are in danger in our own element") to a major one ("then how much more so if we leave it!"), called in Hebrew a *kal ve-homer*. This is one of the early principles of interpretation that were adopted in part from Greek forms.[35] The parable and the logical principle of interpretation in this passage were both techniques that rabbinic literature shared with the cultures around it, but both were adapted for use in learning Torah. The Rabbis here argue that if we are vulnerable when we are immersed in the waters of Torah, how much the more so will we be endangered if we abandon the water for what seems to be a safer environment, the dry land.

In fact, even when Rabbis like Akiva were persecuted and killed by the Romans for disobeying their prohibition, they nevertheless saw Torah as the guarantor of their future. The Torah is "your life and the length of your days," meaning that even though you may be persecuted in this world, you will be rewarded in the world to come. Even though you may be killed as a result of Torah study and observance, the Jewish people as a whole will continue to survive.

Gaining Insights into Our Own Lives

The Rabbis were correct: No Jewish community ever survived if it wasn't engaged in some way with Torah study in the broadest sense. This is surely true of the American Jewish community and its hope for revitalization,[36] as well as for our own personal search for meaning. It is through our own dialogue and struggle with the texts of our collective past, as we work through the Torah, Midrash, Talmud, and Commentaries, that the texts come alive and live through us.[37]

This is especially true of studying the Written Torah, the Five Books of Moses themselves. When we are able to immerse ourselves in the fabric of the biblical narrative—as the modern critic James Kugel has written, "finding some way of dwelling, as it were, in biblical reality"[38]—then the meaning of the text can bring out that which had been previously sealed in us.[39] Reading our sacred texts forces our self-involvement and self-reflection. Thus, with every story we study, we learn not only about the text we are reading but also about ourselves. In deciphering a text, we bring to the fore elements of our own being of which we may not always be conscious. We respond to our own questions and dilemmas.[40] This can happen because the Torah addresses common core experiences that occur in the lives of all human beings at different times.[41]

We generally think of Moses as a character who is larger than life, far beyond our own existence, a redeemer of the Jewish people, warrior, poet, lawgiver, and mystical figure who saw God face to face. But if we pay close attention to the narratives about him, even he can teach us much because of his own frailty. When, following Moses' encounter with the Divine at the Burning Bush, God decides to send him back to Egypt to free his people, Moses responds most simply, "Who am I that I should go to Pharaoh?" (Exodus 3:11). Moses' question, *"Mi anokhi"*—Who am I?—resounds across the generations and pierces our hearts and souls. It is the question of every single human being who is confronted with a task that he or she feels incapable of handling. There are moments when each of us feels just like Moses—when we lack confidence, are reluctant to act, when we even feel like impostors. I remember well when I began teaching at the Hebrew Union College–Jewish Institute of Religion in New York, fresh from our Ph.D. program in Cincinnati in 1975. Though I had passed my comprehensive exams and was in the throes of completing my Ph.D., I knew in my heart of hearts what I didn't know. Those first weeks of teaching were marked by my fear—and it was tangible—that my students would ask me some difficult questions and in so doing expose my utter ignorance. I labored before each class to anticipate every single possible question that could be asked in an effort to deal with the tremendous insecurity I felt. *Mi anokhi*—Who am I? Would they realize that I don't know as much as they think I know?

We all face these moments of insecurity and self-doubt, in our professional as well as in our personal lives. We live with what is called the impostor syndrome, when we fear that others will discover that we are not as good, knowledgeable, altruistic, capable, or bright as they think we are. Moses' words ring in our minds, teaching us about who we are in the deepest sense. As we open our ears, eyes, and hearts to the biblical text, the text reflects back the dilemmas and paradoxes of our own lives, the realities of the world of each and every reader.[42]

A midrash in *Avot d'Rabbi Natan*,[43] a commentary on *Pirkei Avot*, underscores this in a most poignant manner:

> The words of Torah are like golden vessels: the more you scour and rub them, the more they glisten and brighten/reflect the face of him who looks at them. So it is with the words of Torah: whenever you repeat them over and over, they glisten and enlighten/reflect *(me'irin)* the face of the one [who studies them], as it says, "The Commandment of the Lord is pure, enlightening *(me'irat)* the eyes" (Psalms 19:9).

This analogy is simple, and its message is clear. Torah does indeed bring light to the one who studies it; the Torah itself is called light *('or)* and is often symbolized by light, whether it is the light of creation, the fire of the Burning Bush, the revelation at Mount Sinai, or even the light hidden for the righteous in the world to come. The midrashic play on the image from the Psalms text is wonderful, too. The vessel reflects the face of the one who rubs it; the more one rubs the vessel, the more clearly his or her face can be seen. This emphasizes that enlightenment comes when we study the Torah text over and over, and its essence lies in the degree to which we are able to see ourselves reflected in it. Through the mirror of Torah we can come to recognize who we are and who we can become.

Torah Study Must Affect How We Live

The study of Torah is meant to be personally transformational; immersion in the texts of the tradition that involves our deepest self-reflection will ultimately lead to change in us.[44] Study for its own sake *(Torah l'shma)* is very important, but the Rabbis emphasize that it must also affect a person's daily life. According to a statement in *Pirkei Avot* attributed to R. Eleazar b. Azariah, a teacher and contemporary of R. Akiva:

> An individual whose wisdom garnered through Torah study is greater than his or her actions as a Jew is likened to a tree whose branches are numerous but whose roots are sparse. As a result, a strong wind can uproot it *('okkarto)* and overturn it. But a person whose works are more abundant than his or her wisdom is like a tree whose branches are few but whose roots are many; so that even if all the winds in the world come and blow against it, it cannot be moved from its place. In addition, it will neither be affected by the heat nor the drought.

What do the natural forces that threaten the tree—the wind and the heat—represent? For the Rabbis living in the second century C.E., following the destruction of Jerusalem, these forces symbolized the nations of the world that threatened and persecuted Israel, in particular Rome. They believed that if they continued to study Torah and, more important, observe the commandments, God would protect them. According to Maimonides' commentary on this verse of *Pirkei Avot*,[45] their actions were symbolized by the roots, since they are the *'ikkar,* the most essential thing. The word *'ikkar* means both "root" and "principle," but it also is the root of the verb *to uproot,* as we see in the first part of the analogy.

That Torah study must culminate in concrete actions, in the observance of the *mitzvot*, is underscored in an important talmudic debate in Tractate *Kiddushin* 40b between R. Akiva and his contemporary R. Tarfon over which is more important, study or practice. In response to Tarfon's claim that practice is greater, Akiva replied that "study is greater because it leads to practice," and the Rabbis affirmed Akiva's position as being authoritative. Study, if it is to be ultimately meaningful, must affect how we live.

This is also seen in a passage from the midrashic compilation *Sifrei Devarim*. In contrast to works like *Vayikra Rabbah,* which is a series of sermons on the weekly portions of Leviticus, *Sifrei Devarim* is what scholars call an exegetic midrash, meaning that it proceeds verse by verse through, in this case, the Book of Deuteronomy, usually containing several comments on each verse. In section *(piska)* 48, we find an interpretation of the verse "For you shall diligently keep *[shamor tishmerun]* all this commandment which I command you, to do it *[la'asotah]*" (Deuteronomy 11:22):

> "Which I command you, to do it": Why did Scripture say this, seeing that it has already said, "For you shall diligently keep [it]"? I might think that once one has kept the words of Torah, he may stop and need not perform them; therefore Scripture goes on to say, "to do it"—the purpose is *to do it.* If one merely learns, he has fulfilled one commandment; if he learns and keeps what he has learned, he has fulfilled two commandments; if he learns *(lamad),* keeps *(shamar),* and performs *('asah),* there is no one more meritorious.[46]

What issue or problem in the text provides the basis for the rabbis' interpretive comment? Our passage here turns on the implicit question of the relationship between *shamar* (keep, preserve) and *'asah* (do, observe). They could be construed as meaning the same thing: to keep is to observe. If this were the case, then our verse from Deuteronomy would be redundant. But the Rabbis believe that no verse of the Torah is redundant, so they emphasize a difference between these words: "To keep" means to preserve in one's memory and does not necessarily imply observance. Having said this, it is clear that the Torah text had to add the phrase "to do it" in order to underscore that studying the commandments and remembering them are insufficient; study has to lead to the observance of the commandments if it is to be totally meaningful. Study of Torah is ultimately realized in transformed living through the observance of the *mitzvot,* both the ritual and the ethical. It has to be a vehicle that will affect how we act in this world.[47]

2

Who Should Study Torah?

The rabbinic tradition emphasizes that since the Torah was given to the whole of the Jewish people at Mount Sinai, including the future generations yet to be born,[1] the obligation of Torah study falls upon all of us. As a way of underscoring this, the Rabbis described three kinds of glory for the Jewish people by saying that Israel wears three crowns: the crown of priesthood, the crown of royalty, and the crown of the Torah.

> The crown of the Priesthood was bestowed upon Aaron, Moses' brother, as it is said: "And it shall be unto [Aaron] and unto his progeny after him, the covenant of an everlasting priesthood" (Numbers 25:11). The crown of royalty was conferred upon David, as it is said: "His seed shall endure forever, and his throne as the sun before Me" (Psalms 89:37). The crown of the Torah, however, is intended for all Israel, as it is said: "Moses commanded us a law [the Torah], an inheritance for the congregation of Jacob" (Deuteronomy 33:4). Whoever desires can come and make it [his or her] own.[2]

Moses commanded every Israelite, every Jew, to keep the laws of the Torah, including those of all future generations. When the text says, "Moses commanded us (*lanu*)," it is addressed to each and every one of us; we are a part of the congregation of Jacob, the Jewish people, who have inherited the Torah and can make it our own.

Since, according to the Rabbis, every Jew inherits the crown of the Torah, it would seem that each and every Jew should also be obligated to study Torah. But the Rabbis believed that only those who were free and independent could take upon themselves the obligation of Torah study, since observance of commandments such as the study of Torah in essence involves accepting the burden of relationship with God, who is understood to be the Master of the Universe. Torah was given on Mount Sinai, in the openness of the desert, to a generation of Israelites who cast off the yoke of Egyptian slavery. They rejected one master, Pharaoh, in order to accept the "yoke of the commandments," in Hebrew 'ol malkhut shamayim, the yoke of heaven. Therefore, all those who are free are obligated to observe the commandments and study God's words. This, according to the rabbinic tradition, in which women were subject to the dominion of their husbands or other male relatives,[3] excluded women, as it excludes two other categories of individuals: children and slaves.[4] Torah study involves honoring God and is a form of grandeur equal to the priesthood and royalty, and those who are not free individuals cannot be obliged to participate in it.

However, all those who are free and capable of studying Torah are obligated to do so. The tradition makes no distinction between rich or poor, those of sound health or those ill, the young, the old, or the feeble in this regard. Even the poor beggar, who goes from door to door requesting charity, is under the obligation to set aside a definite period of time during the day for talmud Torah (the study of Torah).[5] According to the tradition, it is incumbent on every Jew who possibly can to be immersed in Torah study continually, even one who is already a Torah scholar. He, too, is obliged to devote a third of the day to Torah study.[6] Torah study is a lifetime occupation:

If you have studied Torah in your youth, say not, "I shall not study in my old age." Instead, study Torah at all times, "for you know not which (moment of study) will prosper" (Ecclesiastes 11:6).[7]

This statement by R. Akiva's second-century contemporary R. Ishmael appears in *Avot d'Rabbi Natan*. As always, to understand it we need to examine the biblical context from which R. Ishmael's proof text is drawn. The verse from Ecclesiastes (11:6) is part of a passage that speaks about planting seed: "In the morning sow your seed and in the evening do not withhold your hand, for you know not which will prosper." The analogy in this passage is very powerful: studying Torah is like planting seeds for the future; you can never know which planting will bear fruit. Therefore, you must plant (study) continually, morning and night—in your youth and when you grow old.

It Is Never Too Late to Study Torah

The tradition also stresses through several engaging biographical stories that it is never too late to become immersed in Torah. Not having been exposed to Torah study early in life, even though of course that is the ideal, should not prevent someone from beginning. According to his biographical sketch in the tradition,[8] the important *tanna* R. Eliezer ben Hyrcanus was twenty-eight years old when he came to study with R. Yohanan b. Zakkai at Yavneh,[9] the center of Jewish life after the destruction of the Temple in 70 C.E., not knowing even the most basic customs and prayers.

The archetypal example of a late bloomer in Torah study is none other than R. Akiva, who would become the very embodiment of Torah learning in the second century. In the story of his entry into Torah study,[10] the analogy, or *mashal*, used in the narrative is an important part of the text's message and art.

What were the beginnings of Rabbi Akiva? It is said that when he was forty years old he had not yet studied anything. One time he stood by the mouth of a well and wondered, "Who hollowed out this stone?"[11] It was said to him: "Akiva, have you not read [the verse], 'The waters wear away the stones'" (Job 14:19). Thereupon, R. Akiva drew the inference regarding himself: If something soft can wear down that which is hard, all the more shall the words of Torah, which are as hard as iron, hollow out my heart, which is flesh and blood. He immediately turned to the study of Torah.

He went with his son and sat with an elementary teacher *(melamed tinokot).* He said to him: "Master, teach me Torah." R. Akiva took hold of one end of the [writing] tablet and his son the other end. The teacher wrote down *aleph bet* and he learned it; *aleph tav,* and he learned it [Akiva had to learn the entire Hebrew alphabet, from *aleph* to *tav]*; the Book of Leviticus, and he learned it.[12] He continued studying until he learned the entire Torah.

He then went and sat before R. Eliezer and R. Joshua. He said to them: "My masters, reveal the sense of Mishnah to me" [here, the term is not necessarily a reference to the first code of Jewish law compiled by R. Judah ha-Nasi at the end of the second century, but rather it is understood as referring to all of the Oral Law, the *Torah she-Ba'al Peh*]. When they taught him one *halakhah* [law], he went off to be by himself. "This *aleph,*" he wondered, "why was it written? That *bet,* why was it written? This thing, why was it said?" He came back and asked them, and he reduced them to silence.

R. Akiva, who did not know an *aleph* from a *bet* until the age of forty, was able to master the totality of the tradition. Relatively poor, unlike Eliezer ben Hyrcanus, whose father was one of the wealthiest of the generation, married (to a woman named Rachel), and the father of sons and daughters, R. Akiva nevertheless was willing to sacrifice all for the sake of Torah study. According to the tradition, it took him thirteen years of study before he could begin to teach. For him, as it was for Eliezer and others, immersion in Torah study was the beginning of his life. He was a *tinok*—a young child—a baby, who came to the academy to be suckled and nurtured.

When analyzing this story, we should ask why it emphasizes at the end that Akiva focused upon every *aleph* and *bet*, and probed their meaning. Not only does this show his diligence, but it is consonant with the tradition's picture of R. Akiva and his school as being devoted to the close reading of the Torah and the relevance of each of its elements. Every word, every letter was of ultimate importance. According to the Rabbis, Akiva went on to create innumerable laws and interpretations from each element of text.[13]

In the analogy that underscores Akiva's resolve to learn Torah, it is easy to understand why Torah is compared to water, which fosters growth and fructifies.[14] But why is the Torah described as being "hard as iron"? Perhaps it allows the creator of this tradition to reverse the images in the analogy in a very poignant manner: soft water hollows out the hard stone: therefore, the words of Torah surely can pierce the soft heart of the human being. However, it may also be a way of emphasizing the enduring quality of Torah, which in turn ensures the survival of the Jewish people, who study and live it.

All Can Learn and Teach

The Rabbis emphasize that it is never too late to begin Torah study by shaping powerful models of the most learned and influential leaders who came to Torah study late in life. The message is clear: the average Jew may not achieve the level of learning of R. Akiva, but if Akiva could begin serious study at the age of forty and achieve the success that he did, then nothing should stand in the way of anyone who wants to imbibe the power of the words of Torah. Everyone can study Torah and teach: the old, the young, the rich, and the poor.

The Rabbis further emphasize this in an aggadic passage from the Babylonian Talmud.[15] They pictured a poor person, a rich person, and a sensual person appearing before the heavenly court for judgment, all of whom were asked why they had not occupied themselves with Torah study while they were alive. When the poor person responded that he was worried about his sustenance, they gave the example of Hillel, who was so poor he could not afford to enter the *bet midrash* but climbed the roof to listen through the skylight. To the rich person, who was occupied with his possessions, they described the life of R. Eleazar b. Harsom, who, though exceedingly wealthy, occupied himself with Torah study day and night. And finally, to the sensual person, who claimed that he could not study Torah because he was consumed by his passion (his *yetzer ha-ra,* literally, evil instinct), the Rabbis told the story of Joseph withstanding the seductions of Potiphar's wife.

Torah study is a commandment that applies to all of Israel who are capable of studying. Let us consider the following example from the exegetic midrash on Deuteronomy: *Sifrei Devarim,*[16] compiled in Palestine in the amoraic period, after the close of the Mishnah and before the final editing of the Talmud. This text involves an interpretation of Deuteronomy 11:13: "And it shall come to pass if you harken diligently to My commandments which I command you this day." Because this verse introduces one of the paragraphs of the *Sh'ma,* the credo that Jews say every morning and evening, the writer of this passage could expect readers of *Sifrei Devarim* to be even more than ordinarily sensitive to any nuance in its language that could provide a hook for his interpretation. To explain this verse from Deuteronomy, the midrashist brings as a proof text an apparently unrelated verse, Ecclesiastes 12:11: "The words of the sages are like goads, like nails fixed in prodding sticks *(ba-alei asufot)*. They were given by one Shepherd."

> Based upon what biblical verse do you know that even if
> one learns an interpretation from the least learned [*katan,*
> literally "small"] of the Israelites, he should consider it as if
> he had learned it from a sage? From the verse, "Which I
> command you." And furthermore, it is as if he had learned
> it from many sages, as it is said, "The words of the sages
> are like goads" (Ecclesiastes 12:11).... And furthermore, it
> is as if he had learned it not from many sages, but from the
> [most learned members of the] Sanhedrin, the high rabbinic
> court made up seventy of the most learned sages, as it is
> said, "Masters of assemblies *(asufot)*" (Ecclesiastes 12:11),
> "assemblies" meaning the Sanhedrin, as it is said, "As-
> semble *(esfah)* for Me seventy men of the elders of Israel"
> (Numbers 11:16). And furthermore, it is as if he had learned
> it not from the Sanhedrin, but from Moses, as it is said,
> "They are given from one shepherd" [Ecclesiastes 12:11]....
> And finally, it is as if he learned it not from Moses, but from
> the Almighty One, as it is said, "They are given from *one
> shepherd,*" and "Give ear, O *Shepherd* of Israel, You who
> lead Joseph like a flock" [Psalm 80:2], and "Hear, O Israel,
> the Lord our God, the Lord is *one*" [Deuteronomy 6:4].

So how does the verse from Deuteronomy 11:13, "My commandments which I command you this day," give rise to this
interpretation? The key is the word *you ('etchem)* in the phrase
"which I command *you,*" which is a plural object. The commandments are given to every Israelite. All must observe God's
commandments. Therefore, each person is to study God's words
and teach them. The Torah is given not to special individuals but
rather to the people as a whole. Each Israelite, even if the person is
a *katan* (small), unimportant, limited in learning, can study and

teach, and when this is done, the person is like a learned sage, since the Deuteronomy verse groups all Israelites together: "My commandments which I command *[all of] you*."

The message in the passage then is built upon Ecclesiastes 12:11, citing it to prove each step in the interpretation. The three phrases in the Ecclesiastes text allow the rabbis to expand the meaning to include many sages ("the words of the sages"), the Sanhedrin ("masters of the assemblies"),[17] Moses and God ("one shepherd"). In order for the Ecclesiastes text to work vis-à-vis the Sanhedrin and God, other biblical texts are brought in to smooth the applications. So, in the case of the Sanhedrin, the assembly of seventy judges, the use of the phrase "prodding sticks," *ba'alei asufot,* in Ecclesiastes, is read punningly as "masters of the assemblies (*asufot,* from the verb *asaf,* to gather), and is secured by the citation of the verse from Numbers 11:16: "Assemble *(esfah)* to Me seventy men of the elders of Israel." The assembling of the seventy elders by Moses is seen as a paradigm upon which the later rabbinic Sanhedrin is created. Similarly, in applying the phrase "one shepherd" to God, the Rabbis bring in two proof texts to underscore their point: God is called the "Shepherd of Israel" in Psalm 80:2, and God is described as "one" in Deuteronomy 6:4. The juxtaposing of verses from different places in the Bible that have very different intentions in order to teach is a typical technique used by the Rabbis to teach Torah. It is called intertextuality.[18]

And here their message is powerful, both for the Jews whom they taught and for us. Though each of us may feel *katan* (small) as we contemplate immersion into the breadth and depth of the rabbinic tradition, this passage from *Sifrei Devarim* reminds us that we have the ability to study and even to teach. Even at the outset of our experience of *talmud Torah,* when the weight of the tradition can feel especially overwhelming, the tradition itself reminds us that we indeed can engage in the study of our ancient texts and that our insights themselves can be weighty.[19]

Torah Is within Our Reach

An excellent example of this is found in a passage in *Vayikra Rabbah*,[20] which we learned in chapter 1 is a compilation of sermons built upon the triennial cycle *parashiyyot* (portions) of Leviticus for (each) Shabbat.[21] In *Vayikra Rabbah*, as in all of the homiletic (sermonic) midrashic compilations, the Rabbis frequently use *meshalim*, analogies, usually drawn from their real-life experiences to make their points. Here, the Rabbis underscore their message by comparing Torah to a loaf of bread, while playing on a verse from Proverbs 24:7:

> R. Ammi quoted, "Wisdom is too high for a fool [to attain.]" R. Yohanan said [regarding this]: "This may be compared to a loaf of bread hanging high up in [the rafters of] a house." A fool says: "Who can bring it down?" A wise person says, "Has not someone hung it up? [meaning that if someone hung it high in the rafters, it can also be brought down]. Behold, let me fetch two rods, join them together, and bring it down." So, too, the fool says: "Who can learn the whole of the Torah which is in the heart of a scholar?" Whereas the wise person says, "Has [the scholar] not learned it from another? I shall learn two *halakhot,* two laws, today and two tomorrow until I have learnt the whole Torah like him."

Wisdom—that is, Torah—is compared to a loaf of bread that has been hung high in the rafters of a house in order to be preserved. Since bread is the staff of life in Middle Eastern culture, it is understandable that bread comes to symbolize Torah in this passage. When the loaf of bread seems out of reach, the challenge is to realize that there is a way to grab hold of it. The wise person understands that if someone else has been able to reach so high, that person, too, can find a way to attain his or her goal.

As always, probing the analogy helps us to understand its depth and meaning. The joining of the two rods enables the wise individual to reach far beyond his or her physical limitations. Similarly, by adding two newly learned *halakhot* each day, the student of Torah forms a body of knowledge that extends his or her grasp well beyond its initial capacity. Thus, the student is able to begin to understand Torah and make it a personal passion.

The less-than-clear additional message in this passage is that in order to study Torah seriously, especially at the outset of one's exposure to it, each student needs to find a teacher. Even the *talmid hakham* was at some point the student of a more learned teacher. It is most poignant for us to realize how the term *hakham*, a wise person, is rarely ever used on its own in the rabbinic tradition. The more typical term is *talmid hakham*, literally "a student of one who is wise [in the knowledge of the Torah]." "Wisdom" is indeed equated with Torah, and that is the reason the analogy in this passage is attached to the verse in Proverbs (24:7) cited by R. Ammi: "Wisdom *(hokhmot)* is too high for a fool."

Each According to His or Her Capacity

We have seen how clearly the tradition emphasizes that each person has the ability to study Torah on his or her own level. *Talmud Torah* is a lifetime journey, and each of us is located at a different place—at our own place—on the path of knowledge. The words of Torah are addressed to each one of us in a unique way.

The following midrashic example is found in a homiletic midrash called the *Pesikta d'Rav Kahana*. Like *Vayikra Rabbah*, it is a compilation of sermons that was put together in the late fifth to early sixth century in Eretz Yisrael, the Land of Israel. However, instead of containing sermons on the readings for each ordinary

Sabbath, *Pesikta d'Rav Kahana* contains sermons on the readings for the holidays and the special Sabbaths. There are, for example, specially designated Torah and *haftarah* readings for the Sabbaths before and after Tisha B'Av (the Ninth of Av), which commemorates the destruction of the Temples. This tradition from the *Pesikta d'Rav Kahana* 12:25 is part of a series of interpretations on the first words of the ten commandments (Exodus 20:2): "I am the Lord your God."

As we already have seen a few times, the first question in studying any interpretive text is to establish the connection between the focused text studied and the *derash*, the exposition, of it. In the case of this tradition from *Pesikta d'Rav Kahana*, the reader will have to probe why R. Levi uses the analogy of the statue with many faces in interpreting the opening phrase, *"Anokhi Adonai Eloheikha"* (I am the Lord your God). The key always is to pay attention to every word in the biblical text. In our case, words are used that are different names for God—Adonai and Elohim, which imply different aspects of the Godhead. For the Rabbis, the name *Adonai* symbolizes God's Mercy, and *Elohim*, God's Justice. Even though God is One, represented by the singular *Anokhi* (I), God has many guises. This, then, is the "hook" upon which the following interpretations of R. Levi and R. Yosi bar Hanina are built:

> R. Levi said: The Holy One appeared to them as a statue with faces on every side. A thousand people might be looking at [the statue], but it would appear to be looking at each one of them.
>
> So, too, when the Holy One spoke, each and every person in Israel would say: "The Divine Word is addressing me." Note that Scripture does not say, "I am the Lord your (*eloheikhem*—plural) God," but rather, "I am the Lord your (*eloheikha*—singular) God."
>
> R. Yosi bar Hanina said: The Divine Word spoke to each

and every person according to his or her particular capacity (*kohan,* literally "their strength"). But do not be surprised at this idea. For when manna came down for Israel, each and every person tasted it in keeping with his or her own capacity; infants in keeping with their capacity, young men in keeping with their capacity, and the elderly in keeping with theirs. Thus, for the infants—in keeping with their capacity—since they suckle at their mothers' breasts, they tasted it as their mothers' milk, for it is said: "Its taste is like the taste of rich cream *(l'shad ha-shemen)"* (Numbers 11:8); for young men—according to their capacity—for it is said, "My bread also which I gave you, bread and oil and honey I fed you" (Ezekiel 16:19); and old men according to their capacity, for it is said, "The taste of it was like wafers made of honey" (Exodus 16:31).

Now, what was true about manna—that each and every person tasted it according to his or her own capacity, was equally true about the Divine Word. Each and every person heard it according to his or her own capacity. Thus David said, "The voice of the Lord is in the strength" (Psalm 29:4). [The biblical text does] not say, "The voice of the Lord is in His [meaning God's] strength" [which is what we would expect], but rather, "The voice of the Lord is in [the] strength" [and capacity] of each and every person. Yet, the Holy One said, "[Do not be misled] because you hear many voices, but know that I am He who is one and the same, I am the Lord your God."[22]

God is like a statue that has many sides, and God's word is heard in different ways by different students of Torah. But God, nevertheless, is One.

This passage is made up of three sections, and in each the Rabbis' skill in creating their own meaning and making their own point is the result of their paying close attention to the words of the biblical text. First, in the biblical phrase from Exodus 20:2, "I am the Lord your God," (*eloheikha*—singular), the play on the singular possessive (*your* God) leads the Rabbis to the exact opposite interpretation of the one we encountered above in *Sifrei Devarim* on Deuteronomy 11:13, which turned upon the plural word *you* in the phrase "which I command you."[23] There, the Rabbis stressed that all of Israel was commanded to study God's laws, while here they stress that God's word addresses each individual in a unique way. Each person hears God's word according to his or her own capacity and life situation.

Next, in order to underscore this message, R. Yosi b. Hanina compares God's word to the manna, the miraculous food that the Divine provided for Israel in the desert. Here, as we have seen elsewhere, the Rabbis pun on the plain meaning of the text in order to buttress their message. For example, the phrase from Numbers 11:8, "Its taste was like the taste of rich cream," is used as a proof text about infants who thought that the manna was like their mothers' milk, even though infants are not mentioned at all in the Numbers verse. The Rabbis are able to do this because the Hebrew word translated here as "rich cream," *l'shad*, sounds so much like *shad*, which means "breast." So by aural association, the manna was like mother's milk to infants.

Similarly, in the final section of this passage, the Rabbis find an unusual detail in the language of the biblical text and fine-tune its meaning for their own purpose. The simple understanding of the phrase from Psalm 29:4, "The voice of the Lord is in the strength," is that "the strength" refers to God's strength. But since the verse has no possessive, and therefore does not make this explicit, the Rabbis feel free to read it as if it meant "The voice of the Lord is in the strength [of each person]." The Rabbis are able to read the Torah text in their own way because they themselves are attentive readers.

Finally, all these details build our understanding of why God's word is analogized to the manna that God rained down upon the people. Just as the manna insured the survival of the Israelites on their desert journey from Egypt to the Promised Land, so, too, the words of Torah, heard by each person according to his or her individual capacity, guaranteed the survival of the Jewish people in the days of the Rabbis who framed this midrash and will guarantee it in our day as well. In what way is this so? The answer can be found in the final point in this text: God is One even though we hear the word of God in different ways. God and God's word are one and the same. To study the words of Torah, God's words, is to come in touch with the Divine in the world. Torah study is a gate that opens to divine encounter. And every individual has the capacity to enter the gate of *talmud Torah*.

What Is the Relationship of Women to Torah Study?

As we pointed out at the outset of this chapter, the Jewish tradition is emphatic about Torah study: "Every Jew who is capable is required to study Torah, no matter what his personal circumstances might be, even if he is reduced to the state of begging for charity."[24] Torah study is so important that children were introduced to it by the age of five years,[25] and a Gentile who studies Torah should be considered as holy as the High Priest.[26] Yet, as we learned, women, like slaves and minors, were exempt from this obligation.

What happens, then, if a woman voluntarily studies Torah? The tradition asserts that she will be rewarded, but not in the same measure as a man, since the study of Torah was not imposed upon her as an obligation. In contrast to our own modern idea that an act that comes freely from the heart is somehow "worth more" than one that is obligatory, the Jewish tradition values the commandments so much that it assumes a greater reward for one who acts to discharge an obligation than for the person who performs the identical deed without having been obligated to do so. But even if a woman were to gain some spiritual recompense for the study of Torah, the Rabbis asked whether a man should teach his daughter Torah, and the answer they gave was strident: The majority of women do not have intelligence adequate for Torah study, and, because of their limitations, they will make the words of Torah trivial. "He who teaches his daughter Torah, it is as if he taught her *tiflut,* wantonness."[27] At best, the rabbinic tradition is thoroughly ambivalent about women studying Torah because of their perception of women as acquisitions, and the dominant voices up until the modern period tended to attempt to exclude women from the study of Torah altogether.

There are, however, some notable exceptions.[28] These texts generally hark back to a tradition found in Mishnah *Sotah* 3:4. The Tractate *Sotah* in the Mishnah deals with the laws concerning the suspected adulteress *(sotah)* mentioned in Numbers 5:11–31, who is required to drink water into which this very passage of the Torah has been dissolved. This water ritual is meant to prove the wife's innocence. Following an extensive description of the ritual and the results if the woman is in fact guilty, the Mishnah states:

If she has merit, her merit will mitigate her [punishment].

The most obvious meaning of "If she [the woman] has merit" is probably that she is not guilty of the act for which she is suspected, but that it is not what the Mishnah says. It doesn't say, "And if she is innocent." Rather, it states, "If she has merit." This ambiguity therefore allows the Rabbis to debate what her merit entails.

Ben Azzai said: "A man is obliged to teach his daughter Torah, so that if she drinks [the bitter water], she will know that [her] merit mitigates."

The implication of Ben Azzai's remark is not clear. Does it

mean that the woman's merit is that she studied Torah, and that very act will protect her, or that if she studies Torah, she will learn that she can be protected from the waters of *sotah*? Whatever his intention, he nevertheless does offer a positive comment regarding the teaching of Torah to women, which may not necessarily be restricted to the laws of the *sotah* ritual. However, the Mishnah includes a contrary opinion, seemingly in an attempt to balance Ben Azzai's view:

> Rabbi Eliezer [demurs] and says, "Anyone who teaches his daughter Torah, teaches her *tiflut* [wantonness]."

No. Women do not—or better, should not—study Torah since if they do they will think that they can get away with adultery!

It is surprising that in Mishnah *Sotah,* which has nothing at all to do with *talmud Torah,* Ben Azzai's statement about the teaching of Torah to women is included at all, even though the final editor of this passage contradicts Ben Azzai's point of view with the very negative statement of Rabbi Eliezer.

While the Palestinian Talmud's commentary on *Sotah* indicates that Ben Azzai's comment means that the merit of actually studying Torah is what will stand the suspected adulteress in good stead,[29] this is not the case in the Babylonian tradition. In the following talmudic passage interpreting Ben Azzai's statement in Mishnah *Sotah* 3:4, the possibility that her merit is that of Torah study is rejected out of hand, even though it is mentioned explicitly in connection with the father's obligation to teach his daughter Torah:[30]

> What kind of merit [will mitigate against the suspected adulteress's punishment]? Perhaps we should say, the merit of Torah study, but she is not commanded to do so (though she may do so voluntarily).[31] Therefore, it must mean the merit of [her observing the] commandments. But can the

merit of the commandments protect to such an extent? Have we not learned, "R. Menahem bar Yossi expounded in this way: 'For a commandment is a candle and the Torah is a light'" [Proverbs 6:23]. Scripture compares the commandment to a candle and the Torah to a light, to say to you: Just as a candle only protects momentarily, so does the commandment only protect for a moment [i.e., while it is actually performed], but as a light protects forever, so does the Torah protect forever.

Having rejected the lasting efficacy of the commandments, the Gemara passage does come full circle. Now the rabbis argue that the merit of which Ben Azzai spoke, namely *talmud Torah*, was indeed correct—Torah study will always protect the woman. The symbolism of the candle, to which the commandments are likened, is clear: no matter how large, it burns for only a short time. It has limited power to radiate heat and light. But what about the "light," the *'or* ? As we already have seen, Torah is frequently symbolized by light. However, given its enduring, permanent quality, this is probably an allusion to the light created on the first day of Creation with the words "Let there be light," which according to the rabbinic tradition was then hidden and preserved for the righteous in the world to come.[32] Torah, too, will guarantee ultimate redemption.

But, note how the Rabbis define the woman's involvement in Torah study as this passage continues:

Ravina said: Indeed, [the passage in the Mishnah speaks of] the merit of Torah [study]. And as for what you said that she herself is not commanded to do so—indeed, she is not commanded. But by the merit of her taking her sons to study Torah and Mishnah [i.e., the whole Oral Law] and by waiting for her husband to return from the study house [she is protected].

In an effort to obviate any notion that women are required to study Torah, or are even associated with it, in our passage in the Babylonian Talmud, the Rabbis ignore the possibility that the merit of Torah study protected the suspected wife in her water trial. Instead, they reshape Ben Azzai's statement to mean that it was not the woman's own study but rather her support for her sons and husband in their study of Torah that was her real merit.

Beruriah: A Model of *Talmud Torah*

Although the traditions in the Babylonian Talmud, such as the above interpretation of *Sotah*, generally marginalize women's involvement in *talmud Torah,* even in the Babylonian Talmud's own aggadic portions we find powerful, though limited, examples of women who study and teach. The predominant one is Beruriah, the wife of R. Meir, a leading *tanna* in the generation of Akiva's students.

The following example from Tractate *B'rakhot* 10a turns on a very close reading of the vocalization of one word in a biblical verse. The letters of the Hebrew alphabet are all consonants, and the vowels and other diacritical marks that tell the reader how to pronounce them do not appear in the Torah scroll itself. In fact, the scholars who finalized the pattern of vocalization of the Torah, called the Massoretes, did not do their work until some seven centuries after Beruriah and Rabbi Meir lived. As a result, for the readers of their day, any ambiguity about exactly what word was intended was a potential basis for rabbinic interpretation.[33] Here, in a poignant display of interpretive virtuosity that turns on a single dot in a single letter, Beruriah teaches a moral lesson to her famous husband:

> There were some hooligans in the neighborhood of R. Meir
> who constantly gave him much trouble. R. Meir prayed for

them to die. His wife, Beruriah, said to him: "What is your view, i.e., on what basis do you act this way? Is it because it is written, 'Let the *sinners* be terminated from the earth' (Psalms 104:35)? Does [this verse] say 'sinners' *(hatta'im, from the word hatta')*? [No], it is written, *'sins' (hata'im, from the word hait')*. Moreover, look at the second half of the verse, 'And there are no more evildoers.' [If the first half of the verse means that the wicked people will die, then why the need to mention that there are will be no more evildoers in the second part of the verse? The biblical text would be redundant.] Rather, pray that they repent from their wicked deeds, and then there will be no more evildoers." He prayed for them [as she urged] and they repented.

In this passage, the Rabbis picture Beruriah teaching R. Meir an important lesson based on her textual ability. She focuses on an almost imperceptible vocalization difference in a word in Psalm 104, which forces her erudite husband to recognize that the biblical text must be read thus: "Let the wicked deeds be terminated from the earth, and [as a result], there will be no more evildoers." She seems to know the Bible even better than R. Meir, the greatest teacher of his generation, and as a result, he acts in accordance with her teaching.

Although the thrust of the rabbinic tradition in the Babylonian Talmud and the medieval interpretations of it is to attempt to exclude women from Torah study,[34] there are some strong contrary voices, especially in Palestinian sources, starting apparently with Ben Azzai. On the basis of these dissenting opinions, most segments of Jewish world today, even among the ultra-Orthodox, hold that women are permitted to study at least the Written Torah; and throughout the liberal Jewish community, women are obligated to the same degree as men in the *mitzvah* of *talmud Torah*.

3

Defining Torah

There are many ways to define what Torah is, and many of us subscribe simultaneously to what may be at times even conflicting approaches because they address very different questions. One way is to focus on the textual history of the Bible. Modern scholars have shown that the Bible is made up of diverse literary strands traceable to particular sources that are clearly datable. This "documentary hypothesis"—that the Bible is a sewing together of different literary "documents"—demonstrates the timebound nature of the biblical text. The Torah is the product of individuals who lived in particular eras, and what they wrote reflects the contexts in which they lived.

The Rabbis See the Torah As God's Plan for Human History

The Rabbis, by contrast, were interested in the spiritual and theological meaning of Torah, and consequently they focused on the sense in which the Torah is timeless—literally outside the ordinary sequence of time. For them, it is the blueprint by which God created the world,[1] and therefore it contains every detail of its design. The Torah has all the necessary principles and guiding concepts by which the world will function; even the laws of nature were revealed to Moses at Sinai.[2] The Rabbis stressed the unity of the Torah as the underlying structure of reality,[3] and that all aspects of worldly existence are contained in it. As a result, everything that is known about the world—all past, present, and future occurrences—are a part of the sequence of events in the Torah.[4]

This rabbinic emphasis is most evident in a short passage found in a compilation called *B'reishit Rabbah*. It is one of the most frequently used midrashic texts, and is part of *Midrash Rabbah*. It is like the early exegetic midrashim, such as *Sifrei Devarim,* in that its core is a verse-by-verse treatment of the Book of Genesis. However, it was compiled in Palestine in the fifth century, somewhat later than the exegetic midrashim, and serves as a transition to the later homiletic midrashim in its style, because each of its chapters opens with one or more *petihtaot,* or sermonic introductions. The sermons that make up the homiletic midrashim, such as *Vayikra Rabbah,* are constructed in a three-part form, and the *petihta* is the first part of that form.[5]

The tradition cited in *B'reishit Rabbah* 2:4 interprets a few of the opening verses of the Bible, from the creation narrative (Genesis 1:2–3), as referring to the entire spectrum of history by juxtaposing them with verses drawn from diverse sections of Scripture. As we have noted,[6] this intertextuality is a key element in the creation of midrashic texts:

> R. Shimon ben Lakish interpreted the verses [of the creation story] to speak of the Four Nations [who would persecute the Jewish people in days to come]:[7] "The earth was unformed *(tohu)*" refers to Babylonia, [as we find in the verse] "I beheld the earth and it was unformed *(tohu)*" [Jeremiah 4:23]. "And void *(u-vohu)*" refers to Media (Persia), [as we find in the verse] "They hastened *(yavhilu)* to bring Haman" [Esther 6:14]. "Darkness *(hoshekh)* refers to Greece, which darkened *(heheshikhah)* the vision of the Israelites through its decrees, saying to Israel, 'Write on the horn of an ox that

you have no portion in the God of Israel.'" "Upon the face of the deep"refers to the wicked kingdom [of Rome]: Just as the deep cannot be fathomed, so, too, the wicked kingdom surpasses investigation. "And the spirit *(ruach)* of God hovers" refers to the spirit of the messiah, in accordance with the following verse from Scripture, "And the spirit of the Lord shall be upon him" (Isaiah 11:2).

On account of what will the messiah come imminently? [It will be on account of the merit represented in the verse] "Over the face of the waters"—on account of the merit of repentance, which is likened to water: "Pour out your heart like water" (Lamentations 2:19). R. Haggai [said] in the name of R. Pedat: "There was a covenant made with the water, that even in a time of intense heat, a breeze *(ruach)* will hover over it."[8]

What allows the Rabbis to juxtapose these verses from very dissimilar contexts is the repetition of similar words or grammatical roots. In this tradition attributed to R. Shimon ben Lakish, the Rabbis can identify the phrase "the earth *(ha-aretz)* was unformed *(tohu)*" with Babylonia because the very same words, *"ha-aretz...tohu,"* appear in a passage from Jeremiah describing the destruction in Judea and Jerusalem in 586 B.C.E. as a result of the Babylonian invasion. Similarly, though less obviously, the closeness between the word *vohu* (void) in Genesis 1 and *yavhilu* (they hastened) from the phrase in the Scroll of Esther, "They hastened to bring Haman," allows the Rabbis to identify *vohu* with Media (Persia), since the narrative in the Scroll of Esther takes place there.

Even more subtle is the connection made between "the spirit" *(ruach)* of God hovering, that is, appearing imminent, which is identified with the messiah, and the water creating a breeze *(ruach)* even at a time of intense heat.[9] Making a creative use of the term *ruach* (spirit or wind, breeze), the Rabbis are able to underscore their world-view. The Jewish people in Palestine, from the first century B.C.E. on, suffered under a harsh Roman rule, whose wickedness was unlimited, according to the first part of our passage. And though they believed that God had brought this suffering upon them because of their sins, it was conceivable that it would never end, that is, that Rome would never be defeated. However, the passage goes on to emphasize that redemption (the coming of the messiah) can come at any time if Israel repents. Since repentance is likened to water, Israel needs to "pour out its heart like water," as the writer of Lamentations had declared at the time of the destruction of the Temple at the hands of the Babylonians. No matter how harsh the punishment—even the harshest burning heat (the height of Roman persecution)—water (repentance) can cause a breeze to blow, which will cool and heal. Taken as a whole, this passage views the very creation of the world as anticipating Israel's future suffering under Babylonia, Persia, Greece, and Rome[10] but also as underscoring Israel's ultimate salvation, which will come when Israel repents of her sins and observes God's commandments. Even if Israel publicly disavows its belief in God, which is symbolized in our passage by the writing of such a statement on the horn of an ox, Israel can return to its covenant with God—not by statements of faith but rather by observance of *mitzvot*.

The Torah As Nails Well Planted

The Rabbis believed not only that the Torah given at Mount Sinai anticipated all that would happen in the course of history, but that all new interpretations are an implicit part of the original text. They taught that whatever students will teach in future generations before their own teachers was already given to Moses on Mount Sinai:

> Scripture, Mishnah, *Halakhot,* Talmud, *Toseftot, Haggadot,*
> even that which a faithful disciple would in the future say

in the presence of his master, were all communicated to Moses at Sinai; for it says, "Is there a thing of which it is said: See, this is new?" (Ecclesiastes 1:10). The other part of the [Ecclesiastes] verse provides the reply to this: "It occurred long since, in ages that came before us."[11]

Therefore, the written text and its interpretation are not viewed as totally distinct entities. On the contrary, they were thought to be part of the same revelation. What is deduced from the biblical text is not separate from it, but rather a latent part of it. It is the text within the text.[12] Each midrashic interpreter of a biblical text believes that his or her interpretation makes explicit that which was revealed at Sinai. In a sense, what the tradition tells us is that the revelation of Torah given to Moses is ongoing; the Torah is, at one and the same time, perfect and yet perpetually incomplete.[13] It implicitly contains everything while it is ever expanding.

These seemingly contradictory aspects of Torah are captured in an interesting passage attributed to R. Eleazar ben Azariah, an early second-century C.E. teacher. This tradition, found in the Babylonian Talmud, Tractate *Hagigah* 3a–b, is shaped in the form of a *petihta*, like those found in *B'reishit Rabbah* and the homiletic midrashim. According to some scholars, *petihtaot* such as this one may have actually been preached in some form in the synagogues in Palestine during the rabbinic period,[14] though it is more likely that they are literary constructions.[15] The *petihta*, meaning "opening," most often begins by quoting and then interpreting a verse from the Writings, typically from Psalms, with no obvious connection to the Torah portion read on the particular Sabbath or holiday. Through the artistry of the compiler or the preacher, the opening verse is somehow linked in the end to the first verse of the day's Torah portion, which concludes this "sermonic" piece. This particular *petihta* opens with Ecclesiastes 12:11, and, like the midrash from *Sifrei Devarim* that we read on this same verse, it also includes the phrase "prodding sticks," *ba'alei asufot*, with its alternative meaning of "masters of assemblies."

> [R. Eleazar ben Azariah] opened with: "The words of the wise are as goads, and as nails well planted are the words of the masters of the assemblies, which are given from one shepherd" (Ecclesiastes 12:11).[16]
>
> Why are the words of the Torah compared to a goad? To teach you that just as the goad directs the heifer along its furrow in order to bring forth life to the world, so the words of Torah direct those who study them from the paths of death to the paths of life. But should you think that just as the goad is movable, so the words of the Torah are movable, i.e., impermanent, therefore the text [in Ecclesiastes] says, "[they are like] nails."
>
> But [should you think] that just as the nail neither diminishes nor increases, so, too, the words of the Torah neither diminish nor increase, therefore the text [in Ecclesiastes] says, "well planted"—just as a plant grows and increases, so the words of the Torah grow and increase.
>
> "The masters of the assemblies": these are the sages *(talmidei hakhamim)* who sit in assemblies and occupy themselves with the Torah, some pronouncing unclean, others pronouncing clean, some prohibiting and others permitting, Should a person say: "[In view of the contradictory opinions held by scholars], how can I learn Torah?" Therefore the text [in Ecclesiastes] says, "[All of them] are given from one shepherd." One God gave them, one leader proclaimed them from the mouth of the Lord of all creation, blessed be God, in accordance with the verse, "And God spoke all these words" (Exodus 20:1).

Our first task, as always, is to try to understand the elements of the verse that, because of their amorphousness, either attract the rabbinic comments or are used as a linchpin for the Rabbis. In this passage, the opening verse from Ecclesiastes has several interpretations associated with it because the "the words of the wise"—of course understood as words of Torah—are described in three very different ways: they are compared to both goads and nails and are also described as being "well planted." From these comparisons, one could draw very different conclusions about the nature of Torah: Are the words of Torah movable like the goads, are they fixed like nails, or are they ever changing and growing? These three notions seem contradictory.

However, this is not the case at all, which is underscored by the second half of the passage. Lest you think that because the great teachers, the "masters of the assemblies," offer many seeming contradictory pronouncements, one cannot begin to study and understand God's words, the tradition concludes by quoting the end of the Ecclesiastes passage: "All [these words of Torah] are given from one shepherd"—all of them are a part of Torah, which comes from God, and therefore all are authoritative. Similarly, the Torah and its interpretive process, which has many divergent aspects, all emanate from God.

Our *petihta,* which began with the quotation from Ecclesiastes, ends with the verse that introduces the ten commandments: "And God spoke all these words" (Exodus 20:1). The implication drawn from this verse is that all the seeming contradictory interpretations given by our teachers are a part of Torah. The emphasis in the verse is crucial: God spoke *all these words*—the words of the Scripture as well as the interpretations of all succeeding generations.[17]

Written Torah and Oral Torah: Two Parts of a Whole

The view of the tradition is that the revelation heard at Sinai already included the words of the prophets and sages of every generation, which were to be proclaimed and taught in the future.[18] In other words, the Rabbis viewed the interpretation of the biblical text as the natural development of the text itself. The biblical text, which as we already noted is called the Written Torah, or *Torah she-Bikhtav,* actually contains its own potential interpretation,[19] which is called the Oral Torah, the *Torah she-Ba'al Peh.*[20] This is a major principle in rabbinic Judaism: the two Torahs, the Oral and the Written, are one: they complete each other, and neither is conceivable without the other.[21]

The need for the existence of the Oral Torah is inherent in the very nature of the Torah itself. The laws of the Torah could have been neither understood nor fulfilled even at the moment they were conceived, since, as the tradition knew, "that which is plain in the Torah is obscure, all the more that which is obscure."[22] There are so many gaps in the Torah text—places that lack clarity and even numerous contradictions—that an oral tradition had to have existed or been created simultaneously with the written text, in order to make both the legal and nonlegal parts of the Torah meaningful to those who accepted it. This is true even when it comes to one of the most important biblical injunctions—the observance of the Sabbath. The Torah contains only three proscriptions related to the Sabbath: "You shall not do any kind of work *(melakhah)*" (Exodus 20:10 and Deuteronomy 5:14, among other places), "One shall not leave his domicile *(mimkomo)*" (Exodus 16:29), and "Don't kindle a fire in your dwelling places" (Exodus 35:3). But how were the Israelites to know exactly what specific actions were prohibited on the Sabbath? What actually constituted "work" on the Sabbath? (Only four kinds of work are alluded to in the Bible: plowing, cutting, kindling a fire, and gathering wood). How were they to define their domiciles? How far did they extend? And what constituted the "kindling of a fire"? Questions such as these demonstrate the impossibility of a Written Torah without an Oral

Torah, a body of interpretive traditions that make the Written Torah understandable in the generation in which it was given or created and for all subsequent generations. We must presume that oral traditions arose and circulated long before the Rabbis shaped the thirty-nine categories of work to clarify those things that were forbidden on the Sabbath.[23]

Issues such as these demonstrate the impossibility of a Written Torah without any oral traditions to interpret it. In this regard, the mystics described the Torah as black fire on white fire. The white fire is the Written Torah, in which the forms of the letters are not yet clear, because the forms of the vowels and consonants were created by the power of the Oral Torah, which by contrast is likened to black fire. This black fire is like the ink on a parchment. The Written Torah can become concretized only through the agency of the Oral Torah. Without it, Scripture cannot be understood.[24]

The early existence of the Oral Torah can be traced through numerous traditions found in the *Tanakh* itself: passages in the Prophets and Writings that presume knowledge of traditions not found in the Pentateuch, but that clarify laws found in it;[25] in Jewish literature of the Second Temple period, such as the noncanonical books in the Apocrypha and Psuedepigrapha; in the treatises of Philo of Alexandria and *Jewish Antiquities* of the early historian Josephus; and the early Greek and Aramaic translations of the Bible.

The Torah itself establishes the authority of the *Torah she-Bikhtav* by stating in an oft-quoted passage from Deuteronomy 17:8–11: "If there arises a matter which is too hard for you, you shall turn to the judge that shall be in those days…and according to the sentence which they shall declare to you…according to the law that they will teach you, and according to the judgment of which they shall inform you, you shall act; you shall not deviate from the sentence which they shall declare to you, neither to the right nor to the left." Ironically, it is the Oral Torah that even determines the meaning of these very verses themselves.[26] The Rabbis believed that their oral teachings could give new meanings to the words of Scripture for each generation of readers. Revelation occurred once, according to the tradition, but human learning is perpetual.[27] It is not immutable and fossilized, but rather alive because it can evolve.

One of the best examples in the rabbinic tradition of the concept of the evolution of Torah and the recognition that the interpretations of each generation in a way supersede those of the past, though they are based on them, is found in a talmudic story that juxtaposes Moses and Rabbi Akiva. Found in the Babylonian Talmud Tractate *Menahot* 29b, which generally deals with sacrificial laws, this story struggles with the relative importance of the Written Torah given to Moses on Mount Sinai and the later tradition of the Rabbis, the Oral Torah. The "crowns" referred to in this story still decorate the ritually calligraphed letters of today's Torah scrolls.

> When Moses ascended on high [Mount Sinai], he found the Holy One, blessed be God, sitting and attaching crowns to the letters of the Torah. [Moses] asks Him: "Master of the Universe, who prevents You [from giving me the meaning of the crowns]?" He replied: "Someday in the future, a certain man will appear and Akiva ben Joseph is his name, and he will make heaps of laws and interpretations on every jot and tittle [*kotz*, lit., thorn] [of Torah], i.e., based upon these crowns." [Moses] said to Him: "Master of the Universe, show him to me!" [God] said: "Turn around."[28]
>
> [Moses found himself in Akiva's academy] and he went and sat in the very back [lit., at the end of the eighth row]. But he was unable to understand what they were saying, and he became very distressed. However, when a certain [halakhic] matter came up [for discussion] and the students asked Akiva, "Whence do you know this, i.e., what is your

source?" Akiva replied to them: "This is a teaching from Moses on Sinai." And Moses was mollified.

The Rabbis themselves, just as we do, struggled with their own authority. On one hand, they believed that the further back in time an argument could be traced, that is, the closer to Sinai, the more authority it possesses. Surely, a tannaitic statement must be more reliable than an amoraic one. All the more so does a biblical ordinance, described as being *d'Oraita* (from the Torah), hold more authority than one that is *d'Rabbanan* (of our Rabbis). This is clearly seen in our story when Akiva labels the point of law he taught as *Halakhah l'Moshe miSinai* (a tradition taught to Moses on Sinai), meaning that even though Akiva does not have a biblical verse to point to as a basis for his halakhic statement, he received this tradition orally as being *d'Oraita*.

Yet, at the very same time, Moses is portrayed as not being able to follow the legal discussion taking place among Akiva and his students. Similarly, Moses has no idea what the meaning of the crowns are that are attached to the letters of the Torah. By contrast, not only will Akiva be able to know their hidden meanings, but he will add multiple interpretations to every element of Scripture. Every generation of teachers and students of Torah will add their interpretations, which will take all previous knowledge and insight to new heights. Therefore, we, like our forebears, have the ability and even the responsibility to interpret the Torah anew, thereby adding to the accumulated knowledge of the tradition.

But that is precisely the point of this wonderful story. Though Moses cannot possibly understand the *shakla v'tarya*, the give and take of the discussion, he is mollified when he hears that his words— the Torah, both Written and Oral, which he brought down from his encounter on Mount Sinai—are perceived by Akiva's generation as the basis of their legal rulings. Though the tradition must evolve over time, each student of Torah sees himself or herself as having received the tradition from the teachers before, going all the way back to the moment of revelation at Sinai. The tradition must involve both continuity and innovation.[29]

We have emphasized in our analyses of other passages that it is often crucial for the reader to focus on the choice of words and images in a given tradition. The use of the term *kotz* (thorn) by the Rabbis to mean "every small element of Torah" is instructive. Often, what gives rise to splendid interpretations are small irritants in the Torah text that demand resolution. Elements obviously missing from the narrative, seeming contradictions, literary problems, terms that are not clear—all these textual problems spur students and teachers in every generation to respond, and in doing so they create pearls of wisdom that make the Torah come alive. Each and every seeming problem in the Torah text presents the creative and engaged reader with multiple opportunities for interpretation, just as Akiva created "heaps of laws and interpretations" on each *kotz*.

The Preciousness of the Oral Tradition

Even though the concept of "written" and "oral" point to the relative status of Scripture vis-à-vis the rabbinic tradition,[30] the Rabbis go out of their way to emphasize the supreme importance of the interpretive tradition for Jewish life and survival. It is the Oral Torah that is the ongoing basis of the covenant between God and Israel.[31]

The following passage from *Pesikta Rabbati* 5:1 underscores the preciousness of the oral tradition. *Pesikta Rabbati* is much like *Pesikta d'Rav Kahana*, which gave us the midrash about each person learning according to his or her own capacity.[32] Both are collections of literary sermons for the holidays and special Sabbaths. The *Rabbati* is somewhat later than the *Kahana* (it was compiled in the late sixth to early seventh centuries) and is broader in its conception. It contains sermons that are geared not only to the Torah portions read on these occasions but also to the *haftarot* (the prophetic portions) and the Psalms recited. It also contains halakhic *petihtaot* in addition to regular *petihtaot*, as we found in *Vayikra Rabbah* and the *Pesikta d'Rav Kahana*. These halakhic *petihtaot* begin with a question and answer about Jewish law rather than a quote from Psalms or other texts from the Writings, as we find in the regular *petihtaot*.

This passage (which is not part of the *petihta*) explicates the verse Exodus 34:27, in which God speaks to Moses during the revelation on Mount Sinai: "Write you these words, for according to the tenor of these words I have made a covenant with you." The midrashic point will pun on the phrase "according to the tenor" (in Hebrew *ki 'al pi*), an idiom that could be translated literally "for by mouth," that is, orally.

> R. Judah ben Pazzi stated that these injunctions are clearly indicated by the verse, "The Lord said to Moses: *Write* you these words" which refers to the text given in writing; and by "For according to the tenor [*ki'al pi*, lit., for by mouth, orally] of these words," which refers to the translation [of Scripture] that must be given orally. For, as R. Simon went on to say, the very same verse continues, "I have made a covenant with you." By what means was it made? By means of "Write you these words" and also by means of "For according to the tenor of these words [For these words are by mouth, *ki'al pi,* the word *peh* meaning 'mouth']." If you maintain in written form that which was to remain written, and maintain in oral form that which was meant to be oral, then "I, [the Lord], have made a covenant with you." But if you set down in writing that which was meant to be oral and treat orally that which was meant to be in writing, then I shall not maintain My covenant with you.

Using the very biblical passage that underscores God's covenant with Israel on the basis of Scripture ("Write down these words"), the Rabbis establish the equal importance of the Oral Torah. Typically, what strikes the Rabbis is the parallelism between the phrases in Exodus 34:27: "*Write* you *(k'tov l'kha)* these words" and "For after the tenor *(ki'al pi)* of these words." They see the parallelism because the words *'al pi* are taken by them to mean "*orally*" and therefore signify the oral tradition. Therefore, both the Written Torah and the Oral Torah, which here is symbolized by the Targum, the Aramaic translation of the Bible, are crucial and must be maintained. The relationship between God and the Jewish people is dependent on the preservation of both parts of the tradition.

However, the passage does not end on the note of the equality between the *Torah she-Ba'al Peh* and the *Torah she-Bikhtav*. Another point is added in the name of R. Judah b. R. Shalom. Here, the Mishnah represents the entirety of the Oral Torah:

> [On Mount Sinai], Moses requested [from God] that the Mishnah be given in written form. But the Holy One, Blessed be God, foresaw that the nations would translate the Torah, reading it, say, in Greek, and would declare: "We are Israel; we are the children of God." And Israel would [likewise] declare: "We are Israel; we are the children of God." The scales would appear to be balanced [between the two claims]. Then, the Holy One, Blessed be God, said to the nations: "Why are you claiming that you are My children? I have no way of differentiating other than that My child is he who possesses My secret lore *(misterin)*." The nations will then ask: "And what is Your secret lore?" [God] will reply: "It is the Mishnah [the Oral Law]."[33]

According to the Rabbis, all the nations of the world have access to Scripture and consider it their own. It is only the Oral

Torah, which the Jewish people possesses, that distinguishes it. The Oral Torah, called here the *misterin,* the secret knowledge, is what can preserve Jewish identity and ensure Jewish survival. When Paul and other early Christians spoke of the *mysterion* that the Church possessed—by which they meant the *logos,* God's word—the Rabbis responded polemically by emphasizing that the Jewish people is God's covenanted partner, as evidenced by its unique possession of the oral tradition. It is a subtle play on the Exodus 34:27 text, which solidifies this point and allows the Rabbis to respond to this, their greatest challenge during the first centuries of the Common Era. When God's words in Exodus are "Write you these words, for according to the tenor of these words I have established a covenant with you," we have already seen how the Rabbis read the first part of the verse: "Write you these words, for these words are given orally." Now all they have to do is link the second half of this verse with what follows: "For based upon these words which have been given orally, I have established a covenant with you." The covenant between God and Israel is based on the preservation of the Oral Torah. As important as Scripture might be and as authoritative as it is perceived to be, it is the oral tradition, all of rabbinic interpretation of Torah, that is the basis of Israel's unique position in the world.[34]

Halakhah Can Override Scripture: The Torah Is Not in the Heavens

The importance of the oral tradition is underscored by the fact that in several instances rabbinic law clearly overrides a Torah commandment. Note, for example, the case of a bill of divorce, a *get,* which Scripture instructs must be written on parchment. It is called a *sefer keritut,* literally, "a book of divorce" (Deuteronomy 24:3), and the word *sefer* is always understood to refer to formal writing on parchment. Yet, the accepted rabbinic *halakhah* is that it can be written on any item that is detachable.[35] In the Rabbis' view, Oral Torah can circumvent Written Torah for the sake of making Torah a meaningful and practical part of people's lives.

This is consistent with the interpretation of R. Yohanan and Resh Lakish of Psalm 119:126. The *peshat*—the simple, straightforward meaning of this verse—is "It is a time to act for the Lord; they have overturned *[hayfayru]* Your teaching [Torah]." The verse clearly means, "Because they [Israel] have violated the Torah, it is a time to act on God's behalf." But the Rabbis read it in exactly the opposite way: "When it is time to act for the Lord, overturn your Torah!" The interpretation hinges on the two possible meanings of the verb *hayfayru*. In the *peshat,* it is read as a third-person plural past tense verb—"they overturned"—while in the *derash* of Resh Lakish and R. Yohanan it is understood as an imperative plural: "Overturn!" Reading the Psalms verse in this manner, the Rabbis go on to emphasize: "[Better] that one letter of the Torah be uprooted, i.e., better for the Oral Torah to undo one Torah provision, than the whole Torah be forgotten in Israel."[36]

As a consequence of this, Maimonides ruled as follows:

In an emergency, any duly constituted rabbinic court may cancel the words of Scripture...in order to strengthen the religion and prevent individuals from transgressing the Torah.... If they see a need even to set aside a positive commandment or to transgress a specific Torah injunction in order to bring many back to religion, or to save many Israelites from experiencing grief in other ways, they [the court] may act in accordance with the needs of the hour. Just as the physician amputates a hand or a leg in order to preserve the life, so the rabbinic court may rule at some particular time that a precept of Torah may be transgressed temporarily in order that [the Torah] might be preserved.[37]

In order to underscore the supreme importance of the oral tradition, the Rabbis go so far as to picture God, the Divine author of Scripture, actually studying Torah[38] and even quoting a point of law in the name of a rabbinic authority:

> When Moses went up to the heights of heaven, he heard the voice of the Holy One, Blessed be God, as He sat engaged in the study of the portion about the Red Heifer, citing a law in the name of the [teacher] who stated it: "R. Eliezer taught...Moses said to the Holy One: 'Master of the Universe, the worlds above and below are in Your domain, yet You sit and cite a law ascribed to flesh and blood!'"[39]

Even God seems bound by the interpretations of the sages. And of course it is a God who loves Torah study and interpretation who can encourage learning and make it possible for human beings to be able to change the laws of the Torah that, the Divine put forth![40]

This is evident in a strange talmudic story in which God is pictured as being in a dispute with the angelic Heavenly Academy over a certain purity law. In order to settle the matter, God calls on a fourth-century Babylonian *amora*, Rabbah b. Nahmani, to decide between them. The right of the sages to disagree with God as to the interpretation of Torah texts, in essence to ignore the intentions of the Author, God the Divine Self, and then to have God abide by their textual interpretations, indicates that the Rabbis had a sense that they created their own meaning from Scripture and had every right to do so.[41] The meaning of the Torah text is not found in heaven; rather, it is a product of human beings who, struggling in this world, translate Torah into their own life situations.

The best example of the fact that the tradition is in the hands of flesh-and-blood human beings and is not determined in heaven is the story of *Tanur shel Akhnai*, the Oven of Akhnai.[42] R. Eliezer ben Hyrcanus, an early second-century *tanna*, who, as we noted, came to Torah study later in life[43] but was known for his prodigious learning and memory, argued that the oven was clean and could be used, while all the other sages, led by Eliezer's usual sparring partner, R. Joshua, disagreed:

> On that day, R. Eliezer put forth all the arguments imaginable, but [the other sages] did not accept them. He said to them: "If the law agrees with me, let this carob tree prove it." The carob tree moved one hundred cubits—others say four hundred. They said to him: "No proof can be brought from a carob tree, [i.e., we don't accept it.]" Again he said to them: "If the law agrees with me, let the stream of water prove it." And the stream of water flowed backwards. They said to him: "No proof can be brought from a stream of water." Again he said to them: "If the law agrees with me, let the walls of the *bet midrash* prove it." And the walls of the *bet midrash* inclined *(hi-tu)* to fall. But R. Joshua rebuked [the walls], saying: "When scholars are arguing *(menatzhim)* over *halakhah,* what are you to interfere?" So they did not fall.... Again [R. Eliezer] said to them: "If the law agrees with me, let the heavens prove it." A heavenly voice *(bat kol)* came and said: "Why do you dispute with R. Eliezer, since the law agrees with him in all cases?" R. Joshua arose and said: "It is not in Heaven" [Deuteronomy 30:12]. What is the meaning of, "It is not in heaven?" R. Jeremiah said: "That the Torah had already been given at Mount Sinai. We pay no attention to a heavenly voice, for You have already written in the Torah at Mount Sinai: 'After the majority must one incline *(le-hatot)'* [Exodus 23:2]."
>
> R. Nathan came upon [the prophet] Elijah and asked him: "What did the Holy One, Blessed be God, do at that moment?" Elijah said to him: "He was smiling and said: 'My sons have defeated Me *(nitzhuni),* My sons have defeated Me.'"

This fabulous story demonstrates in a very dramatic fashion not only the Rabbis' negative attitude toward miracles but also their greater concern that Jewish survival is dependent on the community's ability to determine Jewish law and to live by it.

The subtle wordplay on which this message turns is most poignant at the very end of the story, when God is portrayed as saying: "My sons have defeated Me *(nitzhuni)*." It is most ironic that God is "defeated" though the Divine is pictured as smiling. And the "defeat" comes as a result of R. Joshua's quoting God's own Torah against the Almighty. Deuteronomy 30:12 states, "It is not in heaven," and accordingly the Torah, which was given by God and ostensibly emanated from heaven, is used to prove that human beings have the authority to determine the law even in the face of Divine intervention. The very Torah verse quoted by R. Joshua as a proof text is used to undermine the authority of continuing revelation. So God does appear to be defeated by His autonomous creation—*natzeah* does mean "defeat," or "conquer." Yet, *netzah,* from the same root, also means "eternity," and even "glory" and "strength." In an alternative verbal form, then, *nitzhuni* could be understood as meaning "they have glorified Me," "they have strengthened Me," or better, "they have made Me everlasting." Read in this manner, the passage shows that God surely was delighted when His creations did exactly what God wanted all along: use Torah to ensure their own survival, and in the process demonstrate their maturity and growth. This is underscored even more by an additional play on the very same Hebrew word *natzah.* R. Joshua rebukes the walls of the *bet midrash*, saying: "When scholars are arguing *(menatzhim)* over the law, what are you to interfere?" Scholarly debate over the law and the meaning of Torah is what ultimately makes God eternal and guarantees their own strength and survival. The human process of interpretation is what is crucial, and no manner of divine intervention can hold a candle to it. What we have is an important axis within the story that highlights the passage's message: that scholars argue *(menatzhim)* over the meaning of Torah demonstrates their autonomous authority and at the same time ensures God's everlasting nature: *nitzhuni banai*— My sons have defeated or eternalized Me.

Another wordplay establishes a second key axis in the story, which also accentuates the meaning embedded in this tradition: that one does not put any stock in the supernatural, but that our understanding of what God demands of us rests with human interpretation and decision making. R. Eliezer, in citing the series of miraculous occurrences to support his point of view, calls upon the walls of the *bet midrash,* which incline *(hi-tu)* to fall to show the correctness of R. Eliezer's position. The verb *hi-tu* comes from the root *n-t-a,* which can mean "to bend," "to turn aside," "to incline," and, in certain constructions, even "to pervert."

The rejection of miracles such as the walls inclining to fall and the emphasis on the key role of collective human interpretation is underscored at the end of the tradition when the verse from Exodus 23:2 using the same word is cited by R. Jeremiah as proof that we do not abide by signs from heaven, but rather follow the majority understanding: "After the majority must one incline *(le-hatot).*" We human beings, in our attempt to fathom what God wants of us and set our course in life, must "turn" *(le-hatot)* to the interpretations of the Torah that are an accepted part of our community; we are *inclined* not to pay attention to miracles, such as the walls of the *bet midrash* inclining, but rather to listen to the interpretations of the teachers and sages of our time.

Torah is what is taught and lived in this world, in our lives; yet, it flows from that which the tradition understands to have been communicated on Mount Sinai more than three thousand years ago.

4

Discovering the Meaning of Torah

To help each of us imbibe the power of the text in order to be touched and transformed by it, we must clarify how the very nature of the biblical text itself presents us with opportunities to find meaning for our lives. In this regard, there is no more important aspect of the Torah narrative than its laconic style.

The Terseness of the Torah Text: Possibilities of Meaning

We have already commented in passing on the gaps in the Torah text and the many places in it that are unclear.[1] But rather than being merely obstacles to overcome, the general lack of details in the biblical narrative presents creative readers of every generation with opportunities for interpretation. As a modern scholar of literary criticism of the Bible, Robert Alter, has written, "It is true enough to say, as [master of literary criticism] Erich Auerbach and others have done, that the sparsely sketched foreground of the biblical narrative somehow implies a large background dense with possibilities of interpretation."[2] Only the crucial, decisive elements of the narrative are provided to the reader; all else is frequently left obscure. Time and place are often undefined and demand interpretation, while thoughts, feelings, and motives remain submerged under the story line.[3] Simply put, the biblical narrative is characterized by its indeterminate nature. Much is not spelled out for us; the text is full of glaring gaps. These include any element in the text that demands interpretation in order to make the story line coherent.[4] They serve to draw the reader into the narrative and to fill in the blanks by adding to the fragments of information supplied by the text. The Rabbis, who see God as the Author of the Torah, naturally view even the gaps in the text as central elements, which must be read and interpreted because they are placed there intentionally. Midrash is the art of entering these interstices, exploring every possible meaning.[5]

The same holds true for each and every lexical or syntactical element in the biblical text. The inclusion of any phrase, word, or even a particular letter can in and of itself be quite important. Since according to the Rabbis, both the Torah text itself and its language are divine, every consonant and vowel is meaningful and subject to interpretation and inference.[6]

A tantalizing example of how the tradition builds a beautiful interpretation based on the presence or absence of a single letter is found in a comment by Rashi on Leviticus 27:42. Rashi was the first of the great European commentators on the Bible. He lived and taught mainly in Troyes, in France, during the eleventh century, but his commentary remains one of the most used and influential throughout the Jewish world to this day. In many editions of the Bible, it is printed right alongside the text. Like most works of this genre, it strove in the main to provide the reader with the *peshat* of the text, its "simple," originally intended meaning. For the most part, his Bible commentary, unlike his equally influential commentary on the Babylonian Talmud, is anthological, collecting and citing earlier traditions found in a variety of midrashim and in both Talmuds. Leviticus 27:42 reads: "Then I will remember My covenant with Jacob; and also My covenant with Isaac; and also My covenant with Abraham I will remember; and I will remember the Land." We would have expected the text to read chronologically: Abraham, Isaac, and Jacob. In fact, this is the only place in the entire Bible where the order of the names of the patriarchs is reversed. Several midrashic comments in a variety of texts underscore the idea that the order is reversed here to stress that these three leaders of the people of Israel are equal: the last, or most recent, generation is as important as the first. Rashi adds that each one's merits ensures Jewish survival. But Rashi has another explanation as well, one that depends on the way the appearance of the Hebrew vowels varies within the Torah text. In this verse, the name of Jacob, *Ya'akOv*, is written "full" *(malei)*, with the optional letter *vav*, depicting the O sound. Rashi comments:

> There are five places [in Scripture] where the name of Jacob is written full, and [coincidentally] there are five places where the name Elijah, EliahU, is written defectively *(haser)* [missing the final *vav*] to intimate that Jacob holds the one letter [the *vav*] in Elijah's name as a pledge that at some future time Elijah will come and announce the redemption of [Jacob's] children, the Jewish people.

Paying attention to the presence of one seemingly extra letter in Jacob's name in this Leviticus verse allows Rashi to create an interpretation that stresses the importance of Jacob, the newest leader of the people of Israel, by taking into consideration the general spelling of the name of Elijah, who is thought of in the tradition as the herald of the messiah. The implication for us is clear. In the chain of leadership of our people, which began with Abraham, the newest link—today's Jacobs, anyone who learns and teaches Torah in our generation—possesses the potential to bring us closer to the fulfillment of our messianic vision.

The Role of the Active Reader

Since every letter of Torah—every *kotz*, as we saw in the story of Moses and Akiva—can be the basis on which an interpretation is created, each element of the text—every word and action, even gaps in the text—possesses potential significance for the reader. The biblical text, especially its occasional raggedness and incoherence, impels readers in every generation to become interpreters using their imagination to derive meaning from it.[7] We are drawn into the narrative, supplying what is meant both from what is said and from what is unsaid by the author. But as the text gains meaning through the reader's response to it, the text may take on greater significance than the author ever intended.[8] Reading and studying the Bible and rabbinic texts is a dynamic interactive process, in which the reader and the text become one, and at that moment meaning is created. The reader is not a passive agent, receiving meaning from the author through the text. Rather, each and every serious, passionate reader is an active participant in the process of creating meaning. A text that is not read has no meaning; it is the reading that determines the meaning.[9] Art not only exists *for* people, but comes *through* them.[10]

Reading a sacred text, especially, forces self-involvement and self-reflection on the part of the reader. When reading Torah, we in effect react to the meaning that we ourselves produce. Since it affects us and our struggle with who we are, we do not simply read the text: we experience it.[11] As we immerse ourselves in the sacred stories of our past we gain a better sense of the meaning of our own baffling personal dramas. This, in turn, can affect our lives and our priorities.[12]

If the text's meaning is the product of the reader's encounter with the text at one point in his or her life, then any interpretation is only one of many possible ways to read that text. Not only does the text address each of us where we are and according to our individual capacities, it may be read differently by us at different stages in our lives and in different circumstances. As we change, so might the way each of us draws meaning from any given text.

The Many Voices and Faces of Torah

The Rabbis emphasized the multivocalic nature of Torah when they said that the Torah has seventy faces.[13] They saw the Torah as a multifaceted jewel, with each element in the text sparkling with many potential meanings. Since their way of encompassing the total world population was to speak of the seventy nations of the world and the seventy languages of humanity,[14] it is clear that when they described the Torah as having seventy faces, the implication was that each and every human being could draw a different meaning from the Torah text. The later mystics speak similarly about the Torah as having 600,000 aspects,[15] a number that echoes the results of the census of the Israelite population taken after the Exodus from Egypt.[16]

Each and every time an individual reader comes to the text a new meaning is created. By paying attention to the various aspects of each biblical text and then juxtaposing them to aspects of other texts, the reader is capable of producing an unlimited number of meanings. This is especially the case because Hebrew verbal forms are fluid—the present tense contains both past and future simultaneously. Any biblical event can therefore be extended indefinitely.[17] Although the creation of the text is finite, that is, we can account for all the literary strands that make up the biblical text, the recreation of the text—its interpretation—is infinite.[18]

A tradition found in Tractate *Sanhedrin* 34a of the Babylonian Talmud is frequently cited to exemplify the infinite voices or meanings inherent in the Torah text. Although Tractate *Sanhedrin* deals mainly with the court system, aggadic traditions like this one are also included in it, as they are in other predominantly legal texts.

The following tradition is taught by Abaye, a fourth-century Babylonian *amora,* who ascribes part of it to the school of R. Ishmael, Akiva's tannaitic argument-partner of two hundred years earlier:

> Abaye answered: For Scripture states: "God has spoken once, twice have I heard this" (Psalm 62:12). One biblical verse may convey many teachings.... In R. Ishmael's school it is taught: "Behold, My word is like fire—declares the Lord—and like a hammer that shatters [a] rock [into many pieces]" (Jeremiah 23:29): just as [a rock] is split into many splinters *[nitzotzot],* so also one biblical verse can be read in many different ways.

This tradition presents the reader with a powerful metaphor: the process of interpretation that "shatters" the word of God, each biblical verse creating multiple meanings. Interpretation energizes the words of the text.

At first blush, the way the Rabbis use the symbols in the Jeremiah text as metaphors seems quite clear: the rock represents the text, while the hammer is the process of interpretation. The hammer shatters the rock, producing many splinters, many different interpretations. This is the way most readers have understood this passage. However, there is an ambiguity here, especially if we focus closely on the words of the Jeremiah verse: "Behold, My word is like fire...and like a hammer that shatters a rock." God's word itself is likened to fire and to a hammer. The hammer seems to represent the text and not the process of interpretation, as most have thought.

The visual image of the hammer as symbolizing God's words—the text itself—is clearer if we look at a parallel tradition found in the Babylonian Talmud *Shabbat* 88a. Here, the same teaching of the school of R. Ishmael is brought slightly differently by another *amora*, the third-century Palestinian teacher R. Yohanan:

> R. Yohanan said: What is meant by the verse, "The Lord gives the word; they that make known the tidings are a great host" (Psalm 68:12)? Every single word that went forth from God was split into seventy languages. The school of R. Ishmael taught: "And like a hammer that shatters a rock [into many pieces]:" just as a hammer is divided into many sparks *[nitzotzot],* so every single word that went forth from the Holy One split into seventy languages.

The key to both of these passages is the hammer that gives off many sparks as it strikes the rock. This image was very common. Some famous teachers themselves earned their livelihoods as smiths, and all would frequently have seen smiths at work wielding their hammers, which, striking the rock or the anvil, would produce what seemed to be an endless shower of sparks. When they looked at the hammer striking the rock, it seemed as if the hammer itself had broken up into many sparks. So, too, God's words embodied in Torah: when interpreted, they give off a multitude of new meanings. And each individual reader, symbolized by the seventy languages, hears the text in his or her own unique way.

Davar Aher: Alternative Meanings Are the Core of Midrashic Interpretation

If multiple interpretations of the Torah text are ever possible, the same can be said for the rabbis' own treatment of Torah. The Midrash (the entire body of rabbinic midrashim) has been described as a cacophony of readings of Scripture that cannot and even should not be harmonized.[19] These sometimes contradictory interpretations of biblical verses stem from the indeterminate nature of the biblical text itself. The Bible's lack of clarity leads the rabbinic readers to create an unending number of interpretations. There is always "another interpretation": a *davar aher*, literally, another word, and the same individual may proffer several of them. For example, R. Hama b. Hanina, in interpreting Genesis 29:2–3, himself offers no fewer than six different interpretations, some of which seem totally different from the others.[20]

Typically, the Midrash does not attempt to smooth over these contradictions. Rather, contradiction and opposition are built into the very structure of rabbinic midrash. And the juxtaposition and arrangement of multiple interpretations of any given text creates a dialogue between the readers of the rabbinic text and the many voices implicit within it.[21] It is as if a conversation is created across generations of rabbinic interpreters, allowing each reader to enter into the debate about the meaning of any particular biblical passage and find his or her personal way of reading the text.[22]

By the early Middle Ages, the idea was already prevalent that any verse can be interpreted in many ways and that all of them can be meaningful, even if they are at times contradictory. For example, Rabbi Eleazer ben Judah of Worms, who lived in the early part of the thirteenth century and wrote a work entitled *Sefer Ha-Hokhmah*, listed seventy-three "Gates to Wisdom" representing seventy-three distinct methods of midrashic interpretation and showed how each functions. In so doing, he demonstrated how different methods can be used to interpret the same verse, thereby producing contradictory meanings, and he was not bothered by this fact. The truth implicit in the Torah text is so rich that it can be revealed in innumerable ways.[23]

The *Pardes:* Four Levels of Interpretation

The mystics of the Middle Ages understood the Torah to be an inexhaustible well that contains many levels of potential meaning, and all the reader needs to do is to find a way to plumb its depth.[24]

These different levels of meaning, or perhaps modes of interpretation, were conventionally divided into four categories, described by the word *PaRDeS*, literally a citrus orchard, which was taken to be an acronym for *Peshat* (literal), *Remez* (allegorical), *Derash* (midrashic), and *Sod* (mystical). The use of this pun on *pardes* is traced to Moses de Leon, the author of the *Zohar*, in the thirteenth century, and later teachers, through the modern period, have frequently used this acronym.[25]

Perhaps this concept of *pardes* was based on an enigmatic story that was shaped in the tannaitic period and was extended in several versions in the Talmuds and in later texts.[26] Each version of the story comes to interpret the notion of the *merkavah*, the mystical chariot described in the opening of the Book of Ezekiel, which is mentioned in Mishnah *Hagigah* 2:1 as one of three biblical passages whose study is potentially harmful and should therefore be restricted. The *merkavah* in this context clearly is a metaphor for any hidden or mystical lore, which the rabbis feel is dangerous.

The earliest (and core) version of the story is found in the Tosefta, a tannaitic interpretation and extension of the Mishnah,[27] in *Hagigah*, chapter 2:3–4. It speaks of R. Akiva and three other rabbis of the early second century. *Aher*, which literally means "the other," is commonly used, as we find here, in place of the name of Rabbi Elisha ben Abuya, because he later became an apostate and left Judaism altogether.

> Four entered the *pardes:* Ben Azzai and Ben Zoma, Aher and Rabbi Akiva. One looked and died; one looked and was smitten; one looked and cut the shoots, i.e., denied the essence of Judaism; and one ascended in peace and descended in peace. Ben Azzai looked and died; about him Scripture states: "The death of [God's] faithful ones is precious in the Lord's sight" (Psalms 116:15). Ben Zoma looked and was stricken; about him Scripture states: "Have you found

honey? Eat what is enough for you" (Proverbs 25:16). *Aher*
looked and cut down the shoots; about him Scripture states:
"Do not let your mouth lead your flesh into sin"
(Ecclesiastes 5:5). R. Akiva entered in peace and left in
peace;[28] about him Scripture states: "Draw me [closer]; we
will run [after you]" (Song of Songs 1:4).

The key to the myriad of interpretations of this tradition
through the ages is the meaning of the term *pardes.* Most rabbinic
scholars have interpreted the term according to its simple meaning
in classical Hebrew: "orchard." The *pardes,* or orchard, however,
is taken as a symbol for a place of dangerous knowledge—perhaps
speculation about the nature of God, which was prevalent among
sectarian groups in the tannaitic period. Understood this way, the
story comes to warn the early students of Torah about the dangers
of immersion into the world of Greek thought. A second possible
interpretation is based on the Greek word *paradeisos,* meaning
"paradise," and this interpretation sees the four rabbis as mysti-
cally ascending to heaven.[29] This way of interpreting the *pardes*
story came to dominate the rabbinic tradition, finding its most extensive expression first in the early mystical texts known as the
Heikhalot literature and then in the later Kabbalistic tradition.

Yet, as we pointed out, by the end of the thirteenth century,[30]
the use of *pardes* to mean speculation about the Torah's meaning
and the four different levels of its interpretation was already in the
air.[31] Perhaps the *pardes* came to represent the process of Torah
study since the Kabbalists understood that the hidden secrets of the
world are apprehended not by mere mystical ascent but rather by
achieving union with God through ever-deepening penetration of
the levels of Torah. Although the Torah needs an outward garment,
made up of its narratives, just as wine, if it is to be preserved, needs
to be bottled, the deeper inner message of Torah lies within. The
tales of the Torah are simply her outer garments, and as the *Zohar*

itself states, "Woe to the person who regards the outer garb as the Torah itself, for such a person will be deprived of a portion in the world to come."[32]

Peshat, Remez, Derash, Sod

The challenge, then, is to understand the different possible levels of analysis of any given biblical text and to know, therefore, that the Torah is truly an unending source of wisdom. The first level of apprehending meaning is the level of *peshat,* from the root *p-sh-t,* which is the simple or plain meaning of a word, phrase, or verse. The *peshat* can be considered the original meaning of the text.

It focuses the reader on the words of the text themselves without any interpretation. The words are all that is important and are to be taken seriously at the outset of study.[33] The rabbis constantly emphasize the importance of understanding the *peshat,* the original meaning of any particular text, as shaped by its context. They underscore this in the famous dictum "No verse can be deprived of its *peshat.*"[34] This is a warning against the tendency to creative interpretation of the text of Torah without holding onto the *peshat.*

One text in which we as readers struggle to hold on to the literal meaning is the Song of Songs. Because of the ease with which one can move to ever deeper levels of interpretation of *Shir ha-Shirim,* which is one of the Five Scrolls and is read on the holiday of Passover, it is easy to overlook the simple beauty and powerful imagery of this love poem. Imbibe for a moment the intensity of the *peshat* of this text through the engaging metaphors used to describe the lovers in the beginning of chapter 2:

> I am a rose of Sharon, a lily of the valleys. Like a lily among thorns, so is my darling among the maidens. Like an apple tree among trees of the forest, so is my beloved among the youths.

Yet, at the very same time, the Rabbis themselves fought against literalism. They said, "If one translates a verse literally, he is a liar!"[35] Although they began with *peshat*, they did not feel compelled to limit themselves to it. On the contrary, they taught us that the *peshat* can be rejected in favor of an interpretation of the biblical text that would underscore the reader's world-view—whether that of Rabbi Akiva in the second century or of a student today—rather than the original meaning of the text.

Remez, meaning "hint" or "allusion," contrastively preserves the surface meaning of the Torah text but adds significantly to it. With *remez,* the words of Torah are frequently transposed to another realm of discourse through being made into metaphor. Through metaphor or allegory, while preserving the words of the text, we learn what the text "is really talking about." This is what Hellenistic writers on allegory refer to as hyponoia, or the "deep sense of the text."[36] The literal meaning and the deeper meaning are not seen by the rabbis as two separate items; the *peshat*, or literal meaning, directs the reader to a deeper level of understanding the Torah text.[37]

Our text from the Song of Songs is a ready-made example of *remez,* since the Rabbis understood the entire scroll as an allegorical description of the mutual love between God and Israel, much as Christianity reads it as speaking of the relationship between Jesus and the Church. The Rabbis' allegorical interpretations of *Shir ha-Shirim* are found in the main in *Shir ha-Shirim Rabbah,* another of the ten works that make up *Midrash Rabbah.* It is thought to have been compiled around the seventh century in Palestine and contains a variety of running comments on the verses of the Song of Songs. The following interpretation of our phrase, "A lily among thorns," will demonstrate the allegorical treatment of this text by the Rabbis:

R. Huna applied [our] phrase to the oppressions of the secular powers. Just as a lily, if situated between thorns, when the north wind blows is bent towards the south and is pricked by thorns, but nevertheless its heart is still turned upwards, so with Israel, although taxes in kind and other tributes are exacted from them, nevertheless their hearts are fixed upon their Father in heaven, as it says in the verse, "My eyes are ever toward the Lord" (Psalm 25:15).[38]

R. Huna, an early *amora* who lived in the third century, equates the thorns with the oppressive power under which the people of Israel were subjugated, namely, Rome. The thorns, which threaten Israel's survival, are also identified with the harsh measures Rome inflicted upon Israel, especially the burden of taxes under which Israel suffered. This interpretation also turns on the nature of the lily, which, though it bends easily in the wind (especially if it is harsh) nevertheless constantly reaches toward the sky.

The *derash* teaches meaning for every age.[39] The term *derash* is based on the root *d-r-sh*, which means "to seek" or "to search out" in reference to the Bible, i.e., to search out and to discern meaning in the biblical text. We see perhaps the earliest usage of this verb in Ezra 7:10: "Ezra dedicated himself to search out the meaning of God's law *(lidrosh et Torat Adonai)*." *Derash*, the method of midrash (from the same root), is, as we have seen already, the dominant mode for the creation of rabbinic literature, both the aggadic literature upon which we have focused and also the legal, or halakhic, midrash, that learns about legal practice from the biblical text. To do this, it focuses on the text, interpreting its structural and thematic elements in creative ways. It can at times juxtapose different biblical verses based on key theme words in order to convey meaning. Also, the words of the text can illumine the reader's life experience, while the reader, in bringing his or her life to bear on a text, can penetrate the human issues implicit in it.[40] *Derash* essentially involves the "reading in" of a meaning different from the text's *peshat*. *Derash* changes the surface meaning, as we find in a midrash on one of the phrases in our very text from the Song of Songs (2:1), "Like a lily among thorns":

> R. Isaac applied this verse to Rebekkah, as it says, "And Isaac was forty years when he took Rebekkah, the daughter of Bethuel, the Aramean, of Padan-aram, the sister of Laban, the Aramean, to be his wife" (Genesis 25:20). If the verse wishes to inform us that she was from Padan-aram, why state that she was the sister of Laban, the Aramean? It is to tell us that her father was a trickster, her brother was a trickster, and all the men of her place were tricksters, but this virtuous one came forth from the midst of them. What does she resemble? A lily among thorns.[38]

This *derash* changes the meaning of the text as it applies it to Rebekkah, praising her for her virtue though she grew up surrounded by evil. It is created by the Rabbis because they note the redundancy in the Genesis verse cited. They ask the simple question, "Why was it necessary for the biblical text to tell us that both Bethuel and Laban were Arameans, and then compound the superfluity by adding that they were from Paddan-aram?" They contend that this additional information comes to underscore that both Rebekkah's father and brother were tricksters, which they learn from the sound play on *arami* (Aramean), which if inverted can read *ram'ai*, meaning "trickster." By reading the text in this manner, the Rabbis were able to accentuate the importance of one of the matriarchs while at the same time elevating Israel over the other nations.

The fourth and final level of studying Torah is *sod* (mystery), the mystical sphere of interpretation, which points to the Kabbalists' sense of the mystery of Divine speech and words.

Sod symbolizes the ultimate and eternal dimension of the text;

it assumes that the Torah text has an inexhaustible depth that in the end leads the reader to an encounter with God.

So, if we look at our beautiful phrase from the Song of Songs through the prism of the *Zohar*, we will quickly understand the profound mystical nature of the Kabbalists' interpretation. The *Zohar*, the core of Kabbalistic writings, is identified with the teachings of R. Akiva's student R. Shimon bar Yohai, though the text itself is the work of the Kabbalist R. Moses de Leon, who lived in the thirteenth century.

> Rabbi Hezekiah began by quoting: "As a lily among thorns." Who is the lily? It is the Assembly of Israel. Just as the lily, which is among thorns, contains both red and white, so the Assembly of Israel contains both Judgment and Mercy. Just as the lily has thirteen leaves, so the Assembly of Israel has thirteen attributes of Mercy, which encompass it on every side. From the moment that Elohim is mentioned, He brought forth thirteen words with which to surround the Assembly of Israel, and to protect her, and then the name [Elohim] is mentioned again."[42]

On the surface, this passage may appear to be speaking about the relationship of Israel and God, but it is directed to a wholly other plane—that of the *sefirot*, the different emanations of God in the world. The ten *sefirot* represent the various aspects of God, the Divine attributes and powers, and each is associated with a wide range of metaphors, from colors and key words to the names of biblical characters. One of the *sefirot* is *Malkhut*, literally, Kingship, which is identified with the Assembly of Israel as well as with the Oral Torah. The name Elohim (God) in the story of Creation, Genesis 1:1, is identified with another one of the *sefirot*, *Binah* (Wisdom), and the thirteen words that intervene between the first mention of Elohim and the second, in Genesis 1:2, represent the thirteen attributes of Mercy that emerged from *Binah* to surround and protect *Malkhut*.[43] These allusions represent just the tip of an iceberg of mystical interpretation, which is unending.

Mystical tradition pictured the Torah as a well that no pitcher (in Hebrew, *kad)* can ever empty.[44] In Hebrew, letters are also used as numbers, with *aleph* equal to one, *bet* equal to two, and so on; and the numerical value, or *gematria,* of the word *kad* is twenty-four. This is taken to mean that the twenty-four books contained in the biblical canon can never exhaust the mystical depth of the Torah, which points to the fullness of the hidden presence of the Divine.[45] But some strands of Jewish mysticism went even further in understanding the unending possibility of meanings in the Torah. For example, Levi of Berdichev, a Hasidic master who lived at the end of the eighteenth century, cited the midrashic interpretation of Isaiah 51:4: "A Torah will go forth from me," which states that God says, "A new Torah will go forth from Me." He feigns surprise at this reading, since it is an article of faith that there is no other Torah besides the one given to Moses. So what does this interpretation really mean? That the white spaces in a Torah scroll also consist of letters, that is, meanings, but we are unable to read them. But in the messianic age, God will also reveal to us the meaning of the white of Torah, whose letters will become visible to us. This is the meaning of "a new Torah will go forth from me."[46]

Intertextuality: The Weaving Together of Different Texts

Whether *pardes—peshat, remez, derash* and *sod—*denotes different exegetical methods or different levels of meaning of any given text, the dominant way Torah has been studied over the centuries is *derash*. Midrash indeed is the most characteristic mode of Torah learning and is the process by which most modern Jews also come to the text.

Midrashic interpretation focuses on individual biblical verses. Yet, what most often characterizes midrashic texts is intertextuality: texts echo, interact with, and refer to one another.[47] The Rabbis believed that each verse of the Bible can in principle be connected with its most distant counterpart, just as it can with the one immediately next to it.[48] Indeed, one could say that everything in Torah is interconnected.

This linkage is what we saw in a passage from *Shir ha-Shirim Rabbah*, back in chapter 1,[49] about the fire that flashed around Ben Azzai as he linked verses together. Ben Azzai's joining of verses together in an effort to teach God's word re-created the original experience of revelation.

Intertextuality lies at the core of Torah learning; when the teacher of Torah weaves verses together in order to convey meaning, he or she imitates what the Divine did on Mount Sinai.

When we study Torah midrashically, the phenomenon of intertextuality is present on two levels at the same time. First and foremost, the Bible is characterized by the interrelationship among various verses and passages. Intertextual interpretation is manifest in the Bible itself;[50] certain verses and sections of the Torah are built upon, extend, or interpret others. For example, note the rules concerning the observance of the Sabbath in Jeremiah 17:21–22:

> Thus says the Lord: Guard yourselves for your own sake against carrying burdens on the Sabbath day, and bringing them through the gates of Jerusalem. Nor shall you carry out burdens from your houses on the Sabbath day, or do any work, but you shall hallow the Sabbath day, as I commanded your ancestors.

These injunctions are clearly based on the language of the ten commandments in Deuteronomy 5:12–14, extending and interpreting it in certain ways.[51] The Bible not only spawned a culture of textual interpretation based on the juxtaposition of verses but was its own first product.[52]

The Rabbis were well aware of the intertextuality within Scripture, and their efforts focused on further combining biblical passages. Thus they created new meanings, exposing the interpretive relationships already evident in the Bible, as well as shaping new ties among verses by revealing linguistic and thematic connections heretofore unrecognized.[53] Meaning is released when we readers foster the interaction among texts—meaning that was not apparent from any of the individual texts within its own context. R. Johanan, an important third-century Palestinian teacher, understood that it was through the connecting of texts that ambiguity is clarified and new meaning is created. He stated: "When a [biblical] passage is not clear, one should use other passages for its clarification."[54]

An excellent example of how verses from different parts of the *Tanakh* can be juxtaposed in order to convey new meaning is found in a passage in the *Mekhilta d'Rabbi Ishmael*.[55] The *Mekhilta* is of the same genre of midrashic literature as *Sifrei Devarim*, a portion of which we analyzed in chapter 1.[56] It is an exegetic midrash, proceeding verse by verse through the Book of Exodus, offering a variety of interpretations of each verse, and like *Sifrei Devarim* it was compiled sometime during the amoraic period (third through fifth centuries) in Palestine. This passage interprets the verse "And you shall keep [the paschal lamb, which was purchased on the tenth of the month—Nisan] until the fourteenth day of the same month" (Exodus 12:6). To this verse about the celebration of Passover at the time of the Exodus from Egypt, R. Matia ben Heresh will compare seemingly unrelated verses from Ezekiel 16, the first of which is quoted in the circumcision ceremony: "When I passed by you and saw you wallowing in your blood, I said to you, 'By your blood you shall live.' Yea, I said to you, 'By your blood you shall live' (verse 6) and 'Your breasts were fashioned and your hair was grown. But you were naked and bare when I passed by you again and saw that your time for love had arrived'" (verses 7–8).

> Why did Scripture require the purchase of the paschal lamb to take place four days before its slaughter? R. Matia ben Heresh used to say: Behold it states: "When I passed by you again and saw that your time for love had arrived." This means that the time has arrived for the fulfillment of the oath which the Holy One, blessed be God, swore to Abraham to deliver his children [from slavery]. But as yet they had no *mitzvot* to perform by which to merit redemption, as it further says, "Your breasts were fashioned and your hair was grown, but you were naked and bare," which means bare of any *mitzvot*. Therefore, the Holy One, Blessed be God, assigned them two *mitzvot,* the blood of the paschal lamb, i.e., the commandment to sacrifice the lamb on the eve of Passover, and the blood of circumcision, which they should perform so as to be worthy of redemption. For thus it is said: "When I passed by you and saw you wallowing in your blood, I said to you: By your blood you shall live...by your blood you shall live..." For this reason Scripture required that the purchase of the paschal lamb take place four days before its slaughter, for the only way one can obtain rewards is through deeds.

What makes this verse from the Book of Ezekiel relevant for our understanding of a passage from Exodus about the paschal lamb? Quoted by R. Matia ben Heresh, a Palestinian teacher of the mid-second century, the Ezekiel 16 passage is taken out of its own context and is used as if the prophet were speaking about Israel in Egyptian slavery. But how do the Rabbis make such a connection between these disparate verses? The intertextuality is created as a result of the image of God passing over Israel ("Now when I passed *[e'evor]* by you"), which recalls God passing over the houses of the Israelites in Egypt in Exodus 12:12 ("I will pass through *[ve'avarti]*"). The same verb, *avar* (pass), is used in both verses. The literary resonance fosters the connection here, and the Rabbis use the emphasis on the "time of love" as a reference to the period following the redemption of Egypt and the trek through the desert toward the Promised Land. The desert journey to Sinai is described in rabbinic literature as the period of the courtship of God and Israel, with the revelation at Mount Sinai seen as the actual wedding.

Israel had matured through all the years of Egyptian captivity but had not as yet shown that it was spiritually mature—according to the passage, they were "bare of the *mitzvot.*" But how could they have observed the commandments when the revelation at Sinai had not occurred? So God gave the Israelites two blood commandments: the sacrifice of the paschal lamb described in Exodus 12 and the act of circumcision already demanded of Abraham in Genesis 17—symbols of ritual identification and the covenant between God and Israel, which they could observe in order to demonstrate their fidelity and worthiness. And when Israel observed these two pre-Sinai *mitzvot,* God again passed over them and saw them now wallowing in their blood, according to Ezekiel 16. Once again, this later prophetic text, which speaks of the time when Israel was in captivity in Babylonia after 586 B.C.E., is understood as describing the actions of the Israelites in Egypt: When God saw the blood of the paschal lamb and their own blood of circumcision, God twice says: "In (through) your blood you shall live," the repetition taken as referring to the two blood rituals. Today, in the ritual of circumcision, the *mohel,* the circumciser, places a drop of wine in the baby's mouth and recites these very words.

The message is clear, especially given the punch line at the end of the passage ("the only way one can obtain rewards is through deeds"): It is the observance of the *mitzvot,* and in particular, the ritual commandments like circumcision, that will ensure the redemption of Israel. It is the willingness of each individual to give his or her own blood that leads to salvation.

When we focus on the interplay between the verses from Exodus and Ezekiel, which refer to two very different historical contexts—slavery under the Egyptians and exile and captivity in Babylonia—and then ask about the message that the Rabbis shaped in response to Roman persecution, the passage is even more powerful. It allows us to move through Jewish history—from Egypt to Babylonia to Rome—as we ostensibly are trying to understand a biblical passage (Exodus 12) that describes the Exodus from Egypt. The Exodus from Egypt is a paradigm that teaches those living under Roman rule in the second century that they will survive, as they have in the past, if they continue to observe God's laws, especially the key ritual commandments that identify them as Jews. In addition, when the early Christian Church emphasized faith over works and rejected Jewish ritual law,[57] the Rabbis had to underscore the primary importance of the *mitzvah* system and circumcision. Christianity emphasized the redemptive power of Jesus' blood alone, but the Rabbis, through their midrashic process, highlighted the power of the blood spilled by each Israelite male.[58]

A Dialogue across the Generations

Midrash, at its core, is a dialogue with the past through interaction with the verses of Scripture. The Rabbis were certainly caught up with the burning issues of their day, chief among which in the talmudic period were the rise of Christianity and subjugation under Roman authority, which led to a battle for Jewish survival. Yet, they expressed their attitudes toward these issues through their wrestling with the verses of Torah.[59]

Torah, in a wider sense, is created through a dialogue with a given biblical text but also through the conversation among generations of interpreters and teachers. Torah emerges dialectically as an ongoing dialogue across time within the religious consciousness of the community of Israel—a dialogue between past, present, and future.[60] When one studies a rabbinic text, therefore, it is important to recognize how the editors have organized a variety of interpretations in a particular sequence. This is especially true of the exegetic midrashim, which at first blush may seem to be nothing more than a potpourri of disparate comments. Yet, upon closer scrutiny, the relationship among comments in a series, often by different teachers from different generations, may not be haphazard. The apparent tensions created by juxtaposing differing interpretations of the same verse may generate new insights and meaning for the reader. By contrast, when two teachers are cited in what seems to be a type of controversy form ("There are two views of this verse; Rabbi A says one thing, while Rabbi B says another"), their views frequently complement each other or define the parameters of an issue.

As contemporary readers we immerse ourselves in this ongoing dialogue with Torah developed over the ages. We not only absorb the meaning of Torah as it reflects the different historic settings in which it is created, but also are able to find our own Jewish souls in the process.[61] As students of Torah defined broadly, at the outset we are required to attempt to understand the intent of the writers of the sacred texts of our people, be it the Bible itself or the writings of our ancient sages. The words of Scripture or of the myriads of midrashim, talmudic commentaries, and codes must be read and analyzed within the contexts in which they were produced. The first question always must be: "What did the compiler or later editor of this passage mean when it was written?" But it is incumbent upon the modern student of Torah to go further. Once we achieve an understanding of the *peshat*—the simple, conventional meaning of the text—modern readers must use the freedom they possess to find their own personal meaning.[62] Postmodern scholars describe this process as "recontextualizing the text." We must not only analyze and study any given text, but then relive it; experience it. The challenge is to see ourselves as part of the centuries-old dialogue about the text, and this occurs when the text and our personal dramas become one.

5

A Community of Learners

In America today we are experiencing a burgeoning of interest in Jewish study by adults. In synagogues, Jewish community centers, seminaries, and retreat centers, more and more courses in Jewish subjects are offered, and most of them are focused upon text study. No longer are entry-level adult education classes sufficient to quench the thirst that exists in the Jewish community for serious study of the texts of our tradition, especially Torah, Talmud, Midrash, and Kabbalah. Individuals want to find personal meaning for their lives. Immersed in a world of materialism, in which we are usually validated by what we possess, and in a generation in which the "I" is primary, we search as serious individuals for ways to feel that each of our lives has ultimate value. One way we can do so is by feeling a part of the *Shalshelet ha-Kabbalah*, the Chain of Tradition that extends back to Sinai and forward to the messianic age. However, as Jews we accomplish this ongoing connection with our people's past as members of a larger community. This, then, is another reason for a return to text: the need to feel a part of a sustaining and embracing community of fellow Jews, all of whom are on Jewish journeys of search for meaning.

Get Yourself a Teacher

Today, we live in the expanding world of the Internet and distance education, in which individuals can gain access to learning opportunities while sitting in the isolation and privacy of their homes, never having to meet fellow students or teachers in person. At times there may be no collaboration of any kind with others, or even direct interaction. Many adult learners are quite comfortable with this kind of individualized experience because it helps them overcome any feelings they may have of anxiety and self-doubt. If they feel illiterate, they can hide behind the computer screen or manual, never having to confront even the teacher. This feeling of embarrassment at a lack of knowledge is surely shared by most adults when they begin to study; at times it even undermines their taking the first step. They will do anything to conceal their perceived ignorance, which they feel acutely as they relate to others who seem to be more knowledgeable.

But this attitude and approach is alien to what Judaism is all about. At the center of traditional Jewish learning is the *chavrutah* (in Ashkenazic Hebrew, *chevrusah)* one's study partner, from the word *chaver,* meaning "friend." No one studies alone in the *bet midrash* or yeshiva. This core concept is evident as early as Joshua ben Perahyah's famous dictum in *Pirkei Avot* 1:6: "Get *(asei)* yourself a teacher *(rav),* [and] acquire *(k'nei)* for yourself a friend *(chaver),* a study companion." Joshua uses the Hebrew imperatives, which indicate both the importance and the difficulty of gaining a teacher and a study partner. *Asei,* from the root *a-s-ah,* meaning "do" or "make," indicates that the prospective students of Torah will have to work hard at finding teachers for themselves, individuals who can direct them to a life of fulfilling God's words. But Joshua ben Perahyah's statement doesn't end there. Each one of us also needs someone with whom to study continually, from whom we can learn in a variety of ways. Therefore the text adds, "Acquire *(k'nei)* for yourself a friend," using the verb *kanah,* also meaning "possess [in perpetuity]." The same verb is used by the Rabbis when a man marries a woman. This, then, indicates to the perceptive reader not only the sense of the enormity of the task but also that one must strive to establish a lifelong relationship with a companion from whom and with whom one can learn Torah.

The importance of learning together is underscored in another passage from *Sifrei Devarim*, one that interprets a verse from Numbers 27 dealing with the announcement of the impending death of Moses and the appointment of Joshua in his stead.[1] *Sifrei Devarim*, which as we have seen is an exegetic midrash on the Book of Deuteronomy, cites and interprets this passage from the Book of Numbers in connection with Deuteronomy 31:14, which also speaks of Moses' death.

> "And the Lord said to Moses: Take for yourself *(kah l'kha)* Joshua, the son of Nun" (Numbers 27:18). "Take for yourself" a man as strong as yourself. "Take for yourself": one can do this only by acquisition *(lekihah)* [i.e., a formal act which is completed when the one acquiring the object takes hold of it in his hand], for one cannot acquire a [study] companion except through great effort, as the Rabbis have said: One should acquire a friend for himself, to study Torah with him, to study Mishnah, i.e., the Oral Law, with him, to eat with him, to drink with him, and to reveal his secrets to him, as it is stated [in Scripture]: "Two are better than one" (Ecclesiastes 4:9), and "A triple cord is not quickly severed" (Ecclesiastes 4:12).

This midrash offers as a sort of double proof text two verses from Ecclesiastes that are a few lines apart. Here is the whole passage:

> Two are better than one, in that they have greater benefit *(sakhar,* literally "reward") from their labor. For should they fall, one can raise the other; but woe to him who is alone

and falls with no companion to raise him! Further, when two lie together, they are warm; but how can he who is alone get warm? Also, if one attacks, two can stand up to him. A triple cord is not readily severed.

Maybe the author of our midrash skipped the intervening verses as a matter of style, or perhaps a later editor, scribe, or printer left them out to conserve parchment or paper. In either case, they would have been confident that we readers would either know the intervening verses or look them up, and we in turn can be sure that the rest of that proof text will have a bearing on the midrash, in one way or another.

Here, several parts of the text from Ecclesiastes can be instructive. First, the word *sakhar* is typically used for the reward we earn for observing the commandments, especially the study of Torah. So when two study together as a *chavrutah,* they will gain great reward from their joint labor. Second, there is also great warmth—heat—generated from the two situated close together, almost as one. Two immersed in Torah, symbolized by fire and light, produce great warmth. Finally, the reader should focus on one obvious question: Why does our text cite the final image of a *triple* cord, when the emphasis in our midrash is on the *two* together? Yet, the Rabbis stressed in *Pirkei Avot* that when two individuals are engaged in Torah, the *Shechinah,* God's immanent presence, is between them.[2] As a cord made of three twisted strands cannot be easily broken, so, too, the covenantal tie between God and Israel is strengthened through Torah study and will never be severed.

Why do the Rabbis focus on the phrase "Take for yourself" *(kah l'kha)*? The word *l'kha,* meaning "to you," offers another hook for reading meaning into our verse from Numbers, since it seems at first glance superfluous: the verse from Numbers 27:18 could have simply read "Take Joshua" instead of "Take *for yourself* Joshua." On the basis of the added word *l'kha,* the Rabbis stress that each student of Torah must find both a study partner and a teacher who are close to him or her. It is not only the teacher's erudition or knowledge that is crucial in Torah study, but the quality of the relationship between the teacher and the student.[3] The same message is sounded by R. Meir: "Study only with someone with whom you are close from the beginning, as it is stated in Proverbs 5:15: 'Drink water from your own cistern, running water from your own well.'"[4] Using our now-familiar comparison between drinking water and imbibing Torah,[5] R. Meir suggests that the Torah that we drink can be supplied only by a person with whom we are close, a soulmate if you will, who can serve as a perpetual source of nourishment. Just as we are totally familiar with every aspect of the well from which we can draw, so our Torah study companion should be someone with whom we share all that is essential.

Immersing oneself in the sea of Torah—Written and Oral—can be overwhelming. It is easy to drown in its waters if we take in too much too fast. So the role of the teacher is also to guide the student in the process, demonstrating how to drink the water little by little so as to be refreshed by it. The way a teacher transmits the concepts of Torah and analyzes its texts will help determine the extent to which the student can develop the skills to learn independently; to be able to find his or her own voice in the text. The aim of the teacher must be to help students draw on their own wellspring of knowledge and meaning, as the Proverbs passage emphasizes, "Drink from your own cistern." The true teacher should not attempt to force the student to accept his or her own views and interpretations of a text, or overwhelm the student with everything he or she knows. Just as the infinite God, according to kabbalistic teaching, had to contract the divine self (a process called *tsimtsum*) in order to make room for the Creation of the finite world, so, too, does the teacher need to limit what is communicated to students to enable them to create their own Torah.[6]

Finding a Community in Which to Study

Part of studying Torah is a search for a community with which to study. Just as revelation occurred as the Israelites stood together as one people on Mount Sinai, hearing God's words for the first time, so the individual's ongoing struggle with the words of Torah must occur within the context of the community. Though it can be very difficult to take the step of becoming part of a study community, the fact is that study within a group can help each learner overcome feelings of anxiety or isolation. The reinforcement we get from fellow students who themselves are on their own Jewish journeys can go a long way in making us feel confident in our own ability. The intellectual stimulation and support gained from being part of a community of learners is crucial.

A wonderful example of this is found in Ecclesiastes *(Mishlei) Rabbah*. This is a relatively late compilation in the *Midrash Rabbah* series, compiled perhaps as late as the tenth century and certainly well after the close of the amoraic period and the final redaction of the Talmud. Like *Shir ha-Shirim Rabbah*, it contains a mixture of midrashic styles and genres. This particular passage happens to concern a group of *tannaim* separated at the time of the destruction of the Temple.

> Rabbi Yohanan ben Zakkai had five students. As long as he was alive, they lived near him. When he died, they all went to Yavneh, except for R. Eleazar ben Arakh, who joined his wife in Emmaus, a wonderful setting with beautiful waters. He waited for the others to come to him, but they did not come. When he saw that they did not come to him, he asked if he could go to them, but his wife would not let him. She said, "Who needs whom?" He replied, "They need me." She said to him, "In the case of a container of food and mice, who goes to whom? Do the mice come to the container of food or does the container go to the mice?" He listened to

her and stayed where he was, until he forgot his knowledge of Torah. A while later the rabbis came to him and asked him a complex legal question, but he did not know how to answer them.[7]

This story emphasizes the importance of being part of a learning community in order to study Torah. According to rabbinic tradition, R. Eleazar ben Arakh was equal in his learning and wisdom to all the others combined.[8] However, without his comrades, R. Eleazar ben Arakh forgot all the Torah he once knew, unable to add to his learning in isolation.

As in many aggadic stories, the core image underscores the Rabbis' message. R. Eleazar's wife seems to compare her husband to the container of food and therefore expects his fellow students to come to him, just as the mice search out the container of food. She thinks that he possesses the source of sustenance, either the seemingly beautiful physical surroundings of Emmaus or his greater knowledge of Torah, and that the others, like mice, will gravitate to him. He, too, feels that they need his knowledge more than he needs theirs. But what neither R. Eleazar nor his wife realizes is that the other four disciples of Yohanan collectively constitute something that he lacks: a community in which Torah is studied. So actually he needs them more than they need him. They are the container of food—a supportive community of learners, which offers each serious Jew the possibility of gaining the sustenance he or she needs, namely, Torah. Without others, Torah study is weakened; without a community—a "container" to hold and protect the nourishment of Torah—in which to study, one will forget all that one has learned.

There is no better exemplar of this than a passage in chapter 6 of *Pirkei Avot*, a chapter known as *Kinyan Torah*, The Acquisition of Torah, from the same verb *kanah* mentioned above.[9] The entire chapter focuses on Torah study.

R. Yose b. Kisma said: Once while I was walking on the road I met a man, who greeted me and I returned the greeting. He said to me, "Rabbi, what place are you from?" I said to him, "I'm from a great city of sages." He said to me, "If it is your pleasure to dwell with us in our place, I will give you a thousand denarii of gold and precious stones and pearls." I replied to him, "My son, if you were to give me all the silver and gold, precious stones and pearls that are in the world, I would not dwell anywhere but in a place of Torah, for when a person departs [from the world], there accompany him neither gold nor silver, precious stones nor pearls, but Torah and good deeds alone, as it is stated: 'When you walk, it will lead you; when you lie down, it will watch over you; and when you awake, it will talk with you'" (Proverbs 6:22).[10]

There is nothing more important in the world than being a part of a community that studies Torah, and nothing more lasting. R. Yose cites the Proverbs passage to prove that it is only the Torah one has learned during one's lifetime that is eternal. But the verse's images further strengthen this message. Walking or journeying, lying down and awakening are understood as representing life in this world, the time of death, and life in the world to come, respectively. R. Yose ben Kisma is stressing that Torah can lead us on our life path, watch over us, and protect us as we depart from this world, and enliven us in the world to come.

Torah l'Shma—Torah for Its Own Sake

From the rabbinic point of view, the study of Torah is its own reward. It is not merely a means to achieving an end, even though according to the rabbinic tradition one who studies Torah for its own sake (l'shma) will indeed experience great reward. This continual stress on Torah study for its own sake and not as a means to an end is seen in the opening section of *Kinyan Torah*, chapter 6 of *Pirkei Avot*, attributed to R. Meir (whom we met with his wife, Beruriah, at the end of chapter 2).

> Whoever occupies himself in the study of Torah for its own sake merits many things; and not only this but [one may even say] that the entire world is considered deserving for his sake. He is called Beloved Companion [of God], who loves the Divine Presence *(ha-Makom)* and loves all creatures, and who makes the Divine Presence glad and makes all creatures glad. And [Torah study] robes him with humility and awe; enables him to be righteous, pious, upright and faithful; and keeps him far from sin and brings him near to merit. And people shall benefit from [his] counsel, discernment, understanding and strength, as it is stated, "Counsel is mine and sound knowledge, I am understanding, I have power" (Proverbs 8:14).... To him are revealed the mysteries of the Torah, and he becomes like an overflowing fountain and like a stream that never ceases to flow; and is modest, patient, and forgiving of insult; and it makes him great and lifts him above the entire creation.[11]

R. Meir's proof text is drawn from Proverbs 8, whose subject is *Hokhmah*, Wisdom, which the rabbis always identify with Torah. Those who study Torah—which, as we have already seen,[12] is described as the water of life, *mayim chayim*—can eventually become fountains overflowing with God's words. They have a sense of God's presence in the world and are full of joy as they live lives of humility and righteousness.

But study for its own sake is not something that our American culture generally affirms. Education is marketed and as a result is seen by most of us as being purposeful—it must lead somewhere.

People study in order to accumulate knowledge and acquire skills that will enable them to find a job, gain a promotion, or enhance their status. Having gained the requisite skills or knowledge, most people have no need to continue their studies in the particular discipline.

Torah study, too, provides us with knowledge and skills. In chapter 1 we read R. Akiva's dictum that the reason Torah study is greater than practice is that it leads to practice. This is certainly an important element of Torah study. But we don't study only the sections of Torah that have practical application in our lives. On the contrary, Torah study, unique among learning, has another, totally different aspect as well. We are all obliged to immerse ourselves in the life-giving waters of Torah for its own sake, *l'shma*. The study of Torah is not seen merely as a means to an end; rather, it is in itself a desired experience and goal, since it brings us close to the Divine. Indeed, God is also pictured as studying the very Torah that He gave to Moses on Mount Sinai.[13] Since God is understood to be omniscient, knowing all, especially the Torah, which was His own creation, God's studying Torah is surely not instrumental in any way. So this portrayal of the Divine by the Rabbis provides us with a powerful paradigm of *Torah l'shma*.

When we immerse ourselves in Torah study, we imitate God and, as a result, cleave to the Divine. This is the ultimate goal of studying God's words—to show our love for God and cleave to God. There is no better example of this than a passage in the Babylonian Talmud, Tractate *Nedarim,* the section that deals with vows. As in all the tractates of both Talmuds, a variety of material finds its way into the discussion by association, and here, on page 62a, we find a powerful call for studying Torah for no other purpose than loving God and strengthening our covenantal relationship with God. The passage comes to interpret Deuteronomy 30:20: "You shall love the Lord your God, listen *(l'shmo'a)* to His voice, that you may cleave to Him":

[This means] that one should not say, "I will read Scripture so that I may be called a sage; I will study so that I may be called Rabbi; I will study in order to be considered an Elder,[14] i.e., a scholar, and sit in the assembly of Elders." Rather, learn out of love, and honor will come at the end, as it is stated: "Bind them upon your fingers, write them upon the tablet of your heart" (Proverbs 7:3), and "Her ways are ways of pleasantness" (Proverbs 3:17), and "She is a tree of life to those who lay hold of her and whoever holds on to her is happy" (Proverbs 3:18).

The Deuteronomy verse is understood in effect as reading: "You will love the Lord your God by listening to His voice, thereby cleaving to the Divine." Imbibing God's words, the words of Torah, is our way of loving God. This is the aim of *Torah l'shma:* We study not for self-aggrandizement but for the sake of drawing closer to the Divine in the world.

The use of Proverbs 7:3 is equally powerful. The opening verses of Proverbs 7 speak especially clearly of *Hokhmah*, Wisdom, which the Rabbis of course understand as Torah:[15]

My child, heed My words; and store up My commandments with you. Keep My commandments and live, My teaching [literally, My Torah], as the apple of your eye. Bind them on your fingers; write them on the tablet of your heart. Say to Wisdom, "You are my sister," and call Understanding a kinsman.

The object is to study and live God's words, and as the phrase "write them on the tablet *(lu'ah)* of your heart" implies, make them an integral part of your being. The allusion is to the two tablets *(luhot)* that God gave to Moses on Mount Sinai, which now must become our inner constitution, not something outside ourselves that we study for any advantages we may gain. The challenge for us is that through our study we must move to the point where each of us can say to Torah, "You are my sister."

All the texts cited from Proverbs try to capture the sheer joy of occupying oneself with Torah. In the eyes of the Rabbis, Torah study is a joy that will, indeed, in the end lead to abundant personal happiness and reward, as promised in Proverbs 3:18: "She is a tree of life to those who lay hold of her and whoever holds on to her is happy."[16] A beautiful parallel passage in *Sifrei Devarim, piska* 48, interprets a verse very similar to Deuteronomy 30:20, in this case Deuteronomy 11:22, which reads, "If, then, you diligently keep all this commandment which I command you, to love the Lord your God, walk in all His ways, and hold fast to Him." The interpretation adds to our sense of the importance and reward for *Torah l'shma*:

> "To love": Study [Torah] for its own sake, and honor will come eventually, for Scripture states, "She is a tree of life to those that lay hold of her" (Proverbs 3:18), "For [the words of Torah] are life to those that find them" (Proverbs 4:22), "She will place on your head a chaplet of grace"—in this world—"a crown of glory will she bestow on you" (Proverbs 4:9)—in the world to come, and "Length of days is in her right hand"—in the world to come—"in her left hand are riches and honor" (Proverbs 3:16)—in this world.[17]

When Torah study is not used for personal gain, in the end it nevertheless will lead to tremendous reward: spiritual riches and reward, which we cannot even fathom when we first taste of the water of Torah. We, like all those who thirst, will be replenished and blessed.

Turn It Over and Over Again

Sifrei Devarim offers another way of interpreting this same biblical verse:

> "If you diligently keep *(shamor tishm'run)* all this commandment which I command you" (Deuteronomy 11:22)—Why was this stated? Because of [the verse], "If you diligently hear *(shamo'a tishm'u)* My commandments" (Deuteronomy 11:13), I might assume that even if one has heard [meaning here "studied"] the words of Torah, he may remain idle and not study them again. Therefore, Scripture here states, "You shall diligently keep," indicating that just as one must be careful not to lose his money,[18] so must he be careful not to lose his learning.[19]

The key part of the proof text, Deuteronomy 11:13, is the phrase *shamo'a tishm'u* ("you shall diligently hear"). The usual translation of this phrase, which is found in any number of biblical passages, is "you shall obey"—that is, doubling the verb for "to hear" means "to obey." It is God's classic conditional statement to Israel: "If you obey My commandments, then I will reward you." However, the root *sh-m-a* literally means "hear," which is understood in our passage as referring to studying. This emerges in an earlier passage in *Sifrei Devarim*,[20] which understands Deuteronomy 11:13 as implying that one is obliged to *study* Torah even when he or she cannot fulfill the commandments, since the words used are *Shamo'a tishm'u*, you shall diligently hear (meaning "listen" or *"study"*).[21] So, on the basis of this verse, one could argue that all one has to do is study the words of Torah once in order to have fulfilled God's commandment.

But the Rabbis want to stress the need to continually study God's words, and they do so by focusing on the words of

Deuteronomy 11:22: "If you shall diligently keep all this command-ment." The only way to keep—meaning "preserve"—God's words is to study them over and over again. If you don't, they will be lost. The phrase *shamor tishm'run* (diligently keep) is like *shamo'a tishm'u,* an infinitive absolute, a grammatical form that is used for emphasis, since in its essence it is built on repetition. The repeti-tion of the verb *sh-m-r,* meaning "to keep," "to guard," and "to preserve," points to our continual activity in order to hold on to Torah and make it our own. We study throughout our lives, re-peating, reviewing, and interpreting anew passage after passage, to make Torah the vehicle that solidifies our relationship with God.

The texts of Torah are worth studying over and over again, as they are an unending source of knowledge. No one can plumb the depth of any one text through a single encounter. In addition, as we change over time we return to texts we have already studied as different human beings, and each engagement with God's words is therefore utterly new and revealing. All of us, no matter how learned we are, benefit from the repetition of text study.

This is a core value in Jewish tradition and is highlighted in no less a text than the *Sh'ma,* the biblical credo, which we recite in prayer several times every day:

> Take to heart these words which I command you this day. Teach them diligently *(ve-shinantam)* to your children. Re-cite them when you stay at home and when you are on your way, when you lie down and when you arise (Deuteronomy 6:6–7).

The key word is *ve-shinantam,* teach them diligently, which is based on the Hebrew verb *sh-n-n,* which can mean "sharpen." But the same word could also have come from the root *sh-n-a,* which variously means "repeat," "teach," and "study." With this association in mind, the essence of the command is for us to study

God's words over and over again. In order for the words of Torah to be sharp, clear, and poignant, they must be repeated constantly throughout the course of our lives. Indeed, the next phrases of the *Sh'ma* heighten this impression: "Recite [the words of God] when you are on your way, when you lie down and when you arise." On a simple *peshat* level, these words represent the whole of daily life: being at home, traveling outside, lying down, and waking up. Yet, the phrasing is the same as we found in the passage from *Kinyan Torah,* in which the words "when you walk," "when you lie down," and "when you awake" are understood as referring to the entire life journey of the individual from birth to death, in this world and the world to come. This Deuteronomy passage can also be understood as symbolically emphasizing that we must study and teach the words of Torah from morning till night, meaning from our youth through our old age, to death and beyond.

This important theme that Torah study is meant for the full cycle of our lives is emphasized by the fact that the Torah is read in the synagogue in an annual cycle, and every year we confront the same portions only to find that they contain new wisdom that we previously had not discovered. Over and over I find myself astonished by some new insight, prompting me to say, "I cannot believe that I never saw this before!" Similarly, the tradition of studying a page of (Babylonian) Talmud daily, the so-called *daf yomi,* results in the Talmud being completed and begun again every seven years.

Whether it be Torah, Talmud, or Midrash to which we are drawn, Ben Bag Bag was correct when he urged us to "Turn it over and over again,"[22] pointing to the unending task and joy of studying the words of God over and over, in order to find out who we are as human beings and Jews, and what God requires of us. This thrust of Ben Bag Bag's dictum from *Pirkei Avot* is clear from the rest of the advice attributed to him:

Turn it over and over, for everything is contained in it; and contemplate it, and grow gray and old over it, and do not stir from it.

Our obligation is to study Torah throughout our lives, even in our old age ("grow gray and old over it"), and never to cease our study.

So we are challenged to devote ourselves to lifelong learning. No matter who we are—young or old, already learned or taking our first steps into the sea of Torah study—we cannot rest on what we have learned at an earlier stage in our lives. If Torah is to continue to have meaning for us, than we have to continually drink in its words. R. Jeremiah said in this regard: "If you studied Torah in your youth, do not say, 'I need not study in my old age,' for you will never know which [moment of study] will be propitious."[23]

Conclusion

Ben Bag Bag's dictum from *Pirkei Avot* to "turn it over and over again" was echoed by a leading actor when he advised film students at the University of Southern California, "Study the Torah—all the best scripts are there. Whatever dramatic device you can dream up, God thought of it first."[1] All that we need to discern a sense of our own life journey and to better understand our own relationships is found in it. The sacred stories of Torah help us gain a sense of ourselves and allow us to feel a part of the life of the Jewish people over time.[2] We know that our lives have meaning when we see ourselves as links in a chain of tradition that extends back to Mount Sinai and beyond as we feel tied to the ultimate power in the universe.

But the question we broached at the outset was, "How is it possible for modern Jews, so immersed in the world of the secular and the material, for whom the words of Torah have lost their sacredness, to find meaning in Torah? How can we come to appreciate the power of God's words and to realize that the messages of the text can touch our souls and give our life ultimate meaning?"

Perhaps Franz Rosenzweig's analysis, written more than sixty years ago, of the modern Jew's relationship with Torah is still true: "We live in new times and the old form of maintaining the relationship between life and the Book will no longer work. Unlike our ancestors, we must discover a new way of Jewish learning.... And it is learning in the reverse order; [learning] that no longer starts from the Torah and leads into life, but [rather] the other way round:

from life, from a world that knows nothing of the law, or pretends to know nothing, back to the Torah."[3]

Many of us are searching for a greater sense of meaning in our lives but come to Torah study with very limited knowledge and exposure to serious Jewish learning. We, who are so cultured in so many different ways, are at the same time novices in the academy of Jewish learning, and that can feel very overwhelming. However, we've tasted a bit of the meaningfulness and joy that comes in drinking from the waters of Torah, and we want more, much more. We are like the impatient convert in the following well-known talmudic story involving the pair of first-century C.E. Palestinian rabbinic leaders Hillel and Shammai:

> It happened that a certain non-Jew came before Shammai and said to him: "Convert me to Judaism on the condition that you teach me the entire Torah while I stand on one foot." Thereupon, [Shammai] drove him away with the builder's cubit which he held in his hand. He came to Hillel, who converted him. [Hillel then] said to him: "What is hateful to you, do not do to your neighbor—that is the whole Torah; the rest is the commentary on that; go and learn it!"[4]

Shammai, thought to have been a builder by profession, happened to be holding a builder's measuring stick in his hand, and he used it to repulse the presumptuous potential convert. But is it sheer happenstance or an intentionally meaningful symbol, since the cubit is used to measure the amount of work done by the builder? For the point seems to be how all students of Torah are to measure what they know and the process by which they are to grow in their knowledge. The study of Torah is a lifelong journey to which we must devote ourselves. There are no easy fixes, only a slow immersion and honing of skills. But when we devote ourselves to ongoing Torah study, we indeed become the builders—those who guarantee the future of our people as we ourselves grow through our learning.

This is captured in the rabbinic wordplay on a verse from Isaiah:

> Peace is so important that it is given to those who study Torah, in accordance with the verse, "All your children *(banai'ich)* are taught of Adonai; great is the peace of your children" (Isaiah 54:13). Do not read the word *"banai'ich"* (your children), but rather *"bonai'ich"* (your builders).[5]

Changing one vowel changes the thrust of the Isaiah passage, enabling the Rabbis to underscore the ultimate importance of Torah study.

It is also interesting to point out that Hillel, in communicating the core of the rabbinic tradition to the potential convert, chose to teach him not the golden rule of Leviticus 19:18: "Love your neighbor as yourself," but its rabbinic version, which is presented in its negative formulation: "That which is hateful to you, do not do to your friend."[6] The rabbis believed that all of Torah learning must lead to action; what is supremely crucial is how we treat other human beings. In the second century C.E., R. Akiva extended Hillel's emphasis on Leviticus 19:18: "'And you shall love your neighbor as yourself'—R. Akiva said: This is the greatest principle of the Torah."[7] Akiva's view presumes that the standard of behavior that each human being expects to experience from others is a sufficient control for how he or she should also act. The individual in this case is the determinant of his or her treatment of others, and this is consistent with Akiva's emphasis on the importance and precedence of the individual human being's sense of what is right.[8]

However, in the same passage, Akiva's younger contemporary Shimon ben Azzai disagrees with the master, arguing in favor of the verses Genesis 5:1–2:

> This is the record of Adam's line. When God created the human being, He made him in the likeness of God—this is a principle even greater than the first!

For Ben Azzai, the determinant of how we should act toward others is the fact that every human being is created in God's image. We ourselves are not the decisive factors, but rather our relationships with the Divine. If we act inappropriately, we do not merely "hurt" others but rather commit a sin. Just as God is always present when words of Torah pass between two people, so, too, God's presence is diminished or enhanced by virtue of how we treat other human beings.

This, then, is the starting point and essence of Torah study: understanding that it both flows from our covenantal relationship with God and at the same time leads us to the divine presence. All the rest is commentary, interpretation, which will help us understand more and more exactly what our relationship with God means and what it requires of us. Torah study will bring each of us to a greater sense of ourselves in relationship to God as it enables us to grow and change on our life journeys.

A poignant example of this is found in a rabbinic interpretation of a seemingly unimportant passage in Exodus, which is set between the crossing of the Red Sea and the revelation at Mount Sinai. Here is what happened immediately after the Israelites crossed the Sea and celebrated God's redemption of the people:

> They went on into the wilderness of Shur; they traveled for three days in the wilderness, but found no water. They came to Marah, but they could not drink the water of Marah because it was bitter; that it is why it is named Marah. And the people grumbled against Moses, saying: "What shall we drink?" So he cried out to Adonai and Adonai showed him a piece of wood [literally, a tree]; he cast it into the water

and the water became sweet. There [God] made for them a statute and ordinance, and there He put them to the test (Exodus 15:22–26).

Imagine this: just three short days before, the Israelites had stepped into the life-giving waters of the Red Sea. They had all the water they needed to cleanse themselves from the Egyptian experience and move toward the Promised Land. Yet, after three days in the heat and the aridity of the desert, all the water was gone. The Rabbis noted that even the fresh water from the springs around the Red Sea that they had taken with them in their water skins had dissipated.[9] Metaphorically, they could not sustain what they had experienced at the Sea. We, too, live in the desert, searching for an oasis, for another poetic moment of uplift and song. We all know what it is to experience the heat of the desert; at times, we all feel lost, and we search for a source of wholeness. And we, like our Israelite predecessors, cannot find water, the source of healing. The midrash points out that the water might have been right under their feet, but they could not find it. Often, the source of our own sustenance is available to us, but we do not have the ability to open our eyes and see it. Our vision is limited by the pain we feel, by the circumstances we struggle to overcome.

And then the Israelites came upon an oasis, a potential source of sustenance, but most ironically the water found there is bitter. What they thought would enable them to survive and flourish turned out to be something other. Similarly, we at times in our search for meaning turn to a variety of quick fixes that turn out to be illusions. And then, in their pain and disillusion, the Israelites complained to Moses for leading them into the arid desert. Moses, not being very experienced in leading this fledgling people, immediately turned to God, crying out to the Divine for help. Uncertain of our faith when we suffer and experience pain, we too cry out to God for some sense of direction, for answers. Confronted by the serious illness of those we love, or suffering from lost dreams or broken promises, we raise our voices in agony.

Then God answered Moses, showing him a tree that would transform the bitter waters. But what kind of tree was it? On the level of *peshat,* maybe there is a type of tree that grows around oases in the desert wilderness and can sweeten water.[10] But the power of the biblical moment demands that we probe the text more deeply on the level also of midrash, of teaching. After all, the Israelites were in the desert, desperately trying to find a way to survive and reach God's mountain and the Promised Land, and we the readers must ask, 'What could ensure their survival?' The Rabbis assist us by pointing out that the text says, "God showed *(va-yoreihu)* Moses a tree," the root of the verb being *y-r-h,* which literally means "teach."[11] The biblical text does not use the similar but more expected word *va-yareihu,* from the root *r-a-h,* meaning "show." What, then, did God symbolically *teach* Moses that could enable his people to survive? What does the "tree"—in Hebrew *'etz*—represent? Of course, it is the *eits chayim,* the Tree of Life, the Torah, which God imparted to Moses, that sweetened the bitter waters of Marah. But why does this rabbinic interpretation work? Because the Rabbis pay attention to what follows in the biblical text: "There He made for them a statute and ordinance, *hok u-mishpat,*" the law, namely the Torah. This is what God gave to the people at Mariah.

Torah can sweeten the bitter waters of our lives; it can facilitate our personal journey from Egypt, *Mitzraim,* the narrow places in our lives (*metzar* in Hebrew is "narrow"), through the aridity of the desert to God's place. Yet, Moses had to use the tree—symbolically for the Rabbis, the Torah—making it his own by casting it into the water in order for it to function. Most assuredly, God could have performed the "miracle," but it was crucial for Moses and the Israelites to use Torah and act themselves. And by doing so, they would survive Egypt, the desert, and all that limited them—

even the harsh Roman persecution under which the Rabbis lived. So we, too, must make Torah our own by bringing ourselves to it and then imbibing the power of each and every word. And our immersion into its life-giving waters must lead to how we live each day, to our observance and ritual practice.

We should note that the ending of the passage is ambiguous: "There He made for them *(lo)* a statute and ordinance, and there He put them to the test *(nisa'hu)*." Both grammatical objects in Hebrew could be read as singular, which sets up the possibility that the text is speaking either about the individual or the people as a whole. Indeed, the ambiguity may be intentional, thereby stressing the tie between the two. We do not relate to the Divine merely as individuals, but rather as members of a people, and our immersion in the waters of Torah comes as part of a wider community of meaning. Our goal must be to help create and then be a part of that larger ongoing community that has struggled with God's words ever since Sinai. It is as part of a community studying and living Torah that we can transform the Wilderness of Shur into a place of God's presence. The word *shur* in Hebrew can mean "to glimpse [into the future],"[12] telling us that even in the midst of the desert we can still sense God's presence and have a vision of the Promised Land. Even in the desert of our own lives, we are not alone; we are a part of a people and feel God's immanence. And we know that there is a force in the universe that makes for wholeness, which can sustain us, which we can come to recognize through the study of Torah, the waters that bring life. "Let all who are thirsty come for water" (Isaiah 55:1).

Notes

Introduction

1. The *Seudah Shelishit* was seen in rabbinic literature as an anticipation of the messianic banquet, in which one of the greatest delicacies was to be the Leviathan, the great fish who would be defeated by the messianic king and consumed. See, in this regard, B.T. *Baba Batra* 74b.
2. See, in this regard, Genesis 48:20.
3. Water is a symbol for several things in rabbinic literature; chief among them is Torah. See, for example, the interpretations of Isaiah 55:1: "Let all who are thirsty come for water."
4. *B'reishit Rabbah* 98 (Vatican ms.).
5. Howard Cooper, "In the Beginning: Chaos, Creation and Theory," *European Judaism* 22 (Winter 1989): 3–4.
6. See, in this regard, Jacob Neusner, *History and Torah: Essays on Jewish Learning* (London: Vallentine-Mitchell, 1965): 14.
7. Torah is referred to by the Rabbis as *mayyim chayim*, living waters.
8. The *Mekhilta d'Rabbi Ishmael, Massekhta d'Vayassa, parashah* 1.
9. See Barry Holtz's poignant comments in this regard in his *Finding Our Way: Jewish Texts and the Lives We Lead Today* (New York: Schocken Books, 1990): 7 (and elsewhere throughout).
10. Stephen Crites, "The Narrative Quality of Experience," *Journal of the American Academy of Religion* 39 (1981): 304.

Chapter 1

1. See, for example, M. *Megillah* 1:8. The term *Ha-Sefarim* is probably very early, as attested to in Daniel 9:2, where it is used in reference to the prophets.
2. Nahum Sarna, "Bible: Canon," *Encyclopedia Judaica,* vol. 4, col. 816.
3. The term appears in Joshua (8:31–32, 23:6) and Kings (1 Kings 2:3 and 2 Kings 14:6, 23:25), though it may not refer to the whole corpus of the Five Books of Moses in these sources.
4. See, in this regard, B.T. *Hagigah* 14a (and elsewhere throughout).
5. Sarna, *Encyclopedia Judaica,* col. 822.
6. M. *Avot* 1:1.
7. Sarna, *Encyclopedia Judaica,* col. 823.
8. E.g., T. *Sotah* 13:2.
9. T. *Yadayim* 2:13.

10. For descriptions of the Oral Torah, see page 57.
11. *Eicha Rabbati Petihta* 2.
12. After describing such duties as honoring one's parents and performing acts of benevolence among the commandments for which there is a reward both in this world and in the world to come, M. *Peah* concludes that the study of Torah is equal to them all.
13. M. *Avot* 6:5. The sixth chapter of *Pirkei Avot* is called *Kinyan Torah*, Acquisition of Torah, and deals at length with the value and characteristics of Torah study. Maimonides, in his *Sefer Mada, Hilkhot Talmud Torah* 3:1, adds that while the crown of the priesthood is given to Aaron and his descendants, and the crown of royalty belongs to David and his progeny, the crown of Torah is available to all of Israel. Every Jew can come and make it his or her own.
14. Maimonides, *Hilkhot Talmud Torah* 3:2. He is quoting here M. *Horayot* 3:8.
15. *Midrash Tanhuma ha-Nidpas Aharei Mot,* 10.
16. For example, B.T. *Behorot* 35b.
17. Jacob Neusner, "Formative Judaism: What Do We Know and How?" *Judaism* 47 (Summer 1998): 334.
18. Susan Handelman, *The Slayers of Moses: The Emergence of Rabbinic Interpretation in Modern Literary Theory* (Albany: State University of New York Press, 1982): 17.
19. Note Jacob Neusner's utilization of this text in his "Formative Judaism," 328–29.
20. In some parallel versions to this tradition, the term *mehayato,* the one who gives him (the child) life, is used and not *maynikato,* his wet nurse.
21. Gershom Scholem, "The Meaning of the Torah in Jewish Mysticism," in *On the Kabbalah and Its Symbolism,* trans. Ralph Manheim (New York: Schocken Books, 1969): 39–42.
22. *Hesed le-Avraham* 11:11, of R. Abraham Azulai, a later kabbalist, as quoted in Michael Fishbane's *The Garments of Torah: Essays in Biblical Hermeneutics* (Bloomington: Indiana University Press, 1989): 35–36.
23. Handelman, *The Slayers of Moses,* 47.
24. *Midrash Shir ha-Shirim Rabbah,* 42.
25. Daniel Boyarin, *Intertextuality and the Reading of Midrash* (Bloomington: Indiana University Press, 1990): 109–10. Boyarin emphasizes the importance of intertextuality, the bringing together of verses from different places in the *Tanakh* as if they address each other or speak of the same focused event. This juxtaposition of verses leads to new insights on the Rabbis' part.
26. For the Rabbis, contiguity means causality. The juxtaposition of two verses is called *semichut,* and it can be used as the basis for teaching.
27. Though the tradition generally takes Horeb and Sinai to be identical, critical scholarship tends to distinguish between them: they are two different mountains, one located in Midian, the other in the Sinai peninsula.
28. *Sifrei Devarim, piska* 49.
29. See, for example, *Sifrei Devarim, piska* 34.

30. B.T. *Sanhedrin* 99b.
31. See Emmanuel Levinas, *Difficult Freedom: Essays on Judaism* (Baltimore: The Johns Hopkins University Press, 1990): 85, as well as Susan Handelman's comments on Levinas' insight, in "The 'Torah' of Criticism and the Criticism of Torah: Recuperating the Pedagogical Moment," in *Interpreting Judaism in a Post Modern Age,* ed. Steven Kepnes (New York: New York University Press, 1996): 234.
32. Maimonides, *The Commandments (Sefer ha-Mitzvot),* vol. 1, trans. Charles Chavel (London: Soncino Press, 1967): 18.
33. Jose Faur, *Golden Doves with Silver Dots* (Bloomington: Indiana University Press, 1986): 60.
34. See, in this regard, David Stern's *Parables in Midrash: Narrative and Exegesis in Rabbinic Literature* (Cambridge: Harvard University Press, 1991).
35. There is an extensive debate about the extent of Greek influence on the formulation of rabbinic rules of interpretation. See, for example, Louis Jacobs, *Studies in Talmudic Logic and Methodology* (London: Vallentine-Mitchell, 1961). There are several classic lists of rabbinic hermeneutical principles (called *middot*), to which the *kal ve-homer* belongs.
36. See Arnold Eisen, "Taking Hold of Deuteronomy," in *Judaism* 47 (Summer 1998): 323.
37. Handelman, "The 'Torah' of Criticism," 230.
38. James Kugel, "Two Introductions to Midrash," in *Midrash and Literature,* ed. Geoffrey H. Hartman and Sanford Budick. (New Haven: Yale University Press, 1986): 88.
39. Wolfgang Iser, *The Act of Reading: A Theory of Aesthetic Response* (Baltimore: The Johns Hopkins University Press, 1980): 157.
40. See, in this regard, my book *Self, Struggle & Change: Family Conflict Stories in Genesis and Their Healing Insights for Our Lives* (Woodstock, Vt.: Jewish Lights Publishing, 1995).
41. Peter Ochs, "Post Critical Scriptural Interpretation in Judaism," in *Interpreting Judaism in a Post Modern Age, 57.*
42. Aviva Zornberg, *Genesis: The Beginning of Desire* (Philadelphia: The Jewish Publication Society, 1995), xii.
43. *Avot d'Rabbi Natan,* version B, chapter 31. There are two recensions of *Avot d'Rabbi Natan,* one of which is found appended to *Seder Nezikin* in the Babylonian Talmud. Both are included in Solomon Schechter's edition republished in New York in 1967. See also Judah Goldin's translation and introduction published by Yale University Press in 1955. Although it is probable that *Avot d'Rabbi Natan* was compiled somewhere between the seventh and ninth centuries, the brunt of its material is much earlier.
44. Holtz, *Finding Our Way,* 29.
45. Maimonides' commentary on the Mishnah, called *Kitab al-Siraj,* is one of the three most used *perushim* on the Mishnah, along with that of Abadiah Bertinoro (1548) and the glosses of Yom Tov Lipmann Heller on Bertinoro. It was written in Arabic and was completed in 1175.

46. The translation is taken from Reuven Hammer's *Sifre: A Tannaitic Commentary on the Book of Deuteronomy* (New Haven: Yale University Press, 1987). These exegetic midrashim are also called tannaitic midrashim, since the tradition believed that they were compiled in the tannaitic period, contemporary with the Mishnah, in the second century. Most of the material found in the tannaitic midrashim does indeed emanate from this period, though the texts were redacted later. See, in this regard, H. Strack and G. Stemberger, *Introduction to the Talmud and Midrash* (Minneapolis, Minn.: Fortress Press, 1996): 269–99.

47. Holtz, *Finding Our Way,* 197. See also B.T. *B'rakhot* 17a.

Chapter 2

1. See, in this regard, Deuteronomy 29:13, which emphasizes that even the future generations of the Jewish people stood before God and committed themselves to the covenant.

2. Maimonides, *Mishneh Torah, Hilkhot Talmud Torah* 3:1.

3. Marriage in rabbinic law falls under the category of *kinyan,* acquisition [of property].

4. The exemption by the Rabbis of three categories of individuals from study—slaves, minors, and women—is the very first legal principle mentioned by Maimonides in the section of his *Mishneh Torah* on the laws of *Talmud Torah* (Chapter 1:1).

5. See, for example, Maimonides, *Mishneh Torah,* 1:8.

6. B.T. *Kiddushin* 30a.

7. *Avot d'Rabbi Natan* version A, chapter 3.

8. See *Pirkei d'Rabbi Eliezer,* chapters 1–2, as well as parallels in *Avot d'Rabbi Natan* A, chapter 6, and B, chapter 13.

9. The version found in *Avot d'Rabbi Natan* A, chapter 6, states that Eliezer was twenty-two years old when he came to Yavne. Perhaps his age is meant as a metaphor for Torah study, since there are twenty-two consonants in Hebrew.

10. *Avot d'Rabbi Natan* A, chapter 6.

11. The word for "hollow," *hakak* in Hebrew, also means "to legislate" or "decree," from the word *hok,* which means "statute" or "law." Therefore, the text underscores the connection between the water hollowing out the rock and the study of Torah.

12. Traditionally, young children *(tinokot)* begin their study of Torah with the book of Leviticus. See, for example, *Vayikra Rabbah* 7:3.

13. B.T. *Menahot* 29a.

14. For water as a symbol of Torah, see page 3.

15. B.T. *Yoma* 35b.

16. *Sifrei Devarim, piska* 41. For more on the exegetic midrashim, see H. Strack and G. Stemberger, *Introduction to Talmud and Midrash,* 266–99.

17. The meaning of the phrase in Ecclesiastes 12:11, "The words of the sages are like...nails fixed in *ba'alei asufot*" is at best uncertain. It could mean "those that are composed in collections" (from *asaf,* to gather) or "prod-

ding sticks" (that which helps to *gather* the animals). The uncertainty of the meaning of *ba'alei asufot* allows the Rabbis to create their interpretation, reading the words literally, "masters of the assemblies."

18. See, in this regard, Daniel Boyarin's important work *Intertextuality and the Reading of Midrash.*
19. Note the poignant comments on this passage by Barry Holtz, in *Finding Our Way*, 32.
20. *Vayikra Rabbah* 19:2.
21. For a description of *Vayikra Rabbah* see page 15.
22. This translation for the most part is based on Barry Holtz' version in his *Finding Our Way, op. cit.*, 88–9.
23. For the interpretation of Deuteronomy 11:13, see page 36–37.
24. See, in this regard, the succinct halakhic statement in Maimonides' *Hilkhot Talmud Torah,* 1:8.
25. M. *Avot* 5:24.
26. B.T. *Sanhedrin* 59a and Sifra *Aharei Mot* 86b.
27. Maimonides, *Talmud Torah,* 1:13. *Tiflut* literally means "foolishness" or "triviality," as is found in *Bamidbar Rabbah* 4:20. Yet, it is more commonly understood as a euphemism for wantonness or lasciviousness, as found in *Midrash* Esther *Rabbah* 3:13.
28. For a creative analysis of some of these key texts and several poignant conclusions that point to the fact that there are significant differences between the Palestinian and Babylonian Talmuds regarding the inclusion of women in *talmud Torah,* see the chapter entitled "Studying Women" in Daniel Boyarin's *Carnal Israel: Reading Sex in Talmudic Culture* (Berkeley: University of California Press, 1993): 167–96.
29. Boyarin, *Carnal Israel*, 172ff.
30. B.T. *Sotah* 21a.
31. Boyarin emphasizes that by the time of the Middle Ages, some texts even prohibit women from studying Torah. See *Carnal Israel,* 174, n. 6.
32. See for example, *B'reishit Rabbah* 3:6. This concept spins on the verse from Psalms 97:11: "Light is sown for the righteous," which is recited in *Kabbalat Shabbat* every Friday night.
33. It is possible that varying vocalization traditions of particular words were known and circulated in different geographic locales. Therefore, when a midrashic interpretation turns on such a difference in a word's vowel pattern, the Rabbis may be playing on differences that actually existed among certain communities.
34. See, for example, Rashi's commentary to B.T. *Avodah Zarah* 18b.

Chapter 3

1. *B'reishit Rabbah* 1:1.
2. *Sifrei Zuta* to Numbers 12:7.
3. Handelman, *The Slayers of Moses,* 39.
4. Ibid., 30.
5. For a description of the tripartite rabbinic homily form found in the homiletic midrashim, see Joseph Heinemann's groundbreaking article, "The

Proem in the Aggadic Midrashim," *Scripta Hierosolymitana* 22 (1971): 100–22.

6. See the comments on the phenomenon of intertextuality on page 38.

7. These four nations (in Hebrew, the *Arba Malkhuyot*) are cited as a paradigmatic group, culminating with Rome, the power under which the Rabbis who shaped these traditions lived.

8. Much of the passage cited here is based on Jacob Neusner's translation of *B'reishit Rabbah* entitled *Genesis Rabbah: The Judaic Commentary to the Book of Genesis: A New American Translation,* vol. 1 (Atlanta: Scholars Press, 1985): 24–25.

9. Note the subtle linguistic play on the phrase "The spirit of God, i.e., the messiah, hovers *(merahefet)* over the face of *(al p'nai)* the waters," symbolizing repentance. The *derash* here reads the phrase as "The messiah will appear imminently because of *(mipnai)* the waters (repentance).

10. Millennialists also emphasize that four wicked kingdoms, symbolized by four beasts, will arise and rule for a thousand years each, and they, too, identify them as Babylonia, Media-Persia, Greece, and Rome. According to their view, the last of these—Rome—takes us to the time of Jesus' First Coming, ushering in a new age. This period will culminate after two thousand years with the Second Coming of Jesus (creating a total schema of world history of six thousand years), which will usher in the full messianic age, the Millennium. The world-view of the Rabbis contrastingly emphasizes that Roman persecution will come to an end and the Days of the Messiah (not Jesus) will begin only when Israel repents for its sins and observes the *mitzvot*.

11. *Vayikra Rabbah* 22:1. See also P.T. *Peah* 6:2 and B.T. *Megillah* 19b.

12. Handelman, *The Slayers of Moses,* 31–41.

13. Ibid., 40.

14. The main exponent of this view is Joseph Heinemann. See, in this regard, his "The Proem in the Aggadic Midrashim," 100–22.

15. R. Sarason, "The *Petihtot* in Leviticus Rabbah: 'Oral Homilies' or Redactional Constructions?" *Journal of Jewish Studies* 33 (1982): 557–67.

16. The meaning of the Hebrew in this verse is uncertain. The new *JPS Hebrew-English Tanakh* (Philadelphia: The Jewish Publication Society, 1999) translates this verse as "The sayings of the wise are like goads, like nails fixed in prodding sticks. They were given by one Shepherd."

17. For similar and instructive interpretation of this passage from Tractate *Hagigah,* see Holtz, *Finding Our Way,* 19–22.

18. Ephraim Urbach, *The Sages: Their Concepts and Beliefs,* translated from the Hebrew by Israel Abrahams (Jerusalem: The Magnes Press, 1975): 304, cites as examples B.T. *B'rakhot* 5a, *Midrash Tanhuma ha-Nidpas Yitro* 11, and *Shemot Rabbah* 28:6.

19. Joel Rosenberg, "Meanings, Morals and Mysteries: Literary Approaches to Torah," *Response* 9, no. 2 (Summer 1975): 71 as quoted by Holtz, *Finding Our Way,* 7.

20. The first time the term *Torah she-Ba'al Peh* is used in the rabbinic tradition occurs in the story of the potential convert who asks the famous

first-century C.E. teacher Shammai how many Torahs there are, and he replies that there are two: the Written and the Oral. This vignette is found in the B.T. *Shabbat* 31a, though it is said that Rabban Gamaliel gave the same reply to the Roman Antonius, which is preserved in *Sifrei Devarim, piska* 351.

21. Gershom Scholem, "The Meaning of the Torah in Jewish Mysticism," 47–48.

22. Judah Halevi, *Kuzari*, 3, 35.

23. M. *Shabbat* 7:2f.

24. Scholem, "The Meaning of Torah," 48–49.

25. See, for example, Nehemiah 8:14ff, which comments on Leviticus 23:42, filling in the gaps in that text's description of the *sukkah,* the booth in which the Israelites dwelt on the holiday of Sukkot, and even uses what seems to be terminology that is almost exegetic (interpretive).

26. Moshe Herr, "Oral Law," *Encyclopedia Judaica,* vol. 12, cols. 1441–42.

27. Fishbane, *The Garments of Torah,* 113.

28. Why did God instruct Moses to "turn around" in order to move into the future to enter R. Akiva's academy? What we seem to have here is a sense of "back to the future." In other words, the future is seemingly behind us, since we cannot see it. It has not yet caught up to us. This is clearly in sync with the Rabbis' sense of history as being circular—the seasons and times repeat continually, with the ultimate repetition being our eventual reexperiencing of *Gan Eden,* the Garden of Eden, as a symbol of the World to Come. It is as if we are stationary and history catches up to us and then passes us by.

29. See the insightful comments of Barry Holtz about this story in his *Finding Our Way,* 23–24.

30. Nevertheless, the blessing recited before the performance of a rabbinic commandment is the same as the one recited before the performance of a biblical commandment. Both are considered divine commands: "Blessed are You, O Lord our God, Ruler of the universe, who has sanctified us with Your commandments and bid us to…." See the comments of David Weiss Ha-Livni, *Peshat and Derash* (New York: Oxford University Press, 1991): 14–15.

31. See, in this regard, the comments attributed to R. Yohanan, the most famous teacher of the third century in Palestine, found in B.T. *Gittin* 60b and *Shavuot* 39a. See also P.T. *Peah* 17c for the difficulty of distinguishing between the Written and Oral Torahs as to their relative importance.

32. See page 40.

33. The translation of this Rabbati passage is based on that of Rabbi William Braude *z"l* in his two-volume translation of *Pesikta Rabbati,* vol. 1 (New Haven: Yale University Press, 1968): 92–93. Braude's translation incorporates material from Parma Ms. 1240 into the *editio princeps* (Prague, 1654).

34. This interpretation is made explicit in P.T. *Peah* 17c.

35. P.T. *Kiddushin* 59d.

36. B.T. *Temurah* 14b.

37. Maimonides, *Yad Hazakah, Hilkhot Mamrim* 2:4.
38. B.T. *Avodah Zarah* 3b.
39. *Pesikta d'Rav Kahana* 4:7.
40. S. Rawidowicz, "On Interpretation," *Proceedings of the American Academy for Jewish Research* 26 (1957): 96.
41. Ha-Livni, *Peshat and Derash*, 160.
42. B.T. *Baba Metzia* 59b.
43. See page 33.

Chapter 4

1. See page 58.
2. Robert Alter, *The Art of Biblical Narrative* (New York: Basic Books, 1981): 114.
3. Erich Auerbach, "Odysseus' Scar," in *Mimesis: The Representation of Reality in Western Literature* (Princeton: Princeton University Press, 1953): 9.
4. Boyarin, *Intertextuality*, 41.
5. Ibid., 40–41.
6. Handelman, *The Slayers of Moses*, 71. We of course noted that the vocalization pattern of the biblical text was finalized only through the work of the Massoretes in the eighth and ninth centuries C.E. in Palestine. See page 48.
7. Meir Sternberg, *The Poetics of Biblical Narrative* (Bloomington: Indiana University Press, 1987): 24, cites Herbert Schneidau, *Sacred Discontent: The Bible and Western Tradition* (Berkeley: University of California Press, 1979).
8. Wolfgang Iser, *The Art of Reading: A Theory of the Aesthetic Response* (Baltimore: Johns Hopkins University Press, 1979): 168.
9. Ha-Livni, *Peshat and Derash*, 158.
10. Iser, *The Art of Reading*, 108. Here, the author quotes Jean Paul Sartre, *Was Ist Literatur?* German trans. Hans Brenner (Hamburg: 1958): 35.
11. Iser, *The Art of Reading*, 128–29.
12. Stephen Crites, "The Narrative Quality of Experience."
13. This concept is found as early as the twelfth century in *Bamidbar Rabbah* 13:15 and then is mentioned in Abraham ibn Ezra's introduction to his commentary on the Pentateuch. It does not appear in the Talmud or in the early midrashim.
14. See, for example, B.T. *Sukkah* 55b and B.T. *Shabbat* 88a.
15. Gershom Scholem, "The Meaning of the Torah in Jewish Mysticism," 65.
16. See, in this regard, Numbers 1.
17. Handelman, *The Slayers of Moses*, 37.
18. J. P. Fokkelman, *Narrative Art in Genesis* (Amsterdam: Van Gorcum, 1975): 3–4.
19. Holtz, *Finding Our Way*, 22.
20. *B'reishit Rabbah* 70:8.
21. Steven D. Fraade, *From Tradition to Commentary: Torah and Its Inter-*

pretation in the Midrash Sifre to Deuteronomy (Albany: State University of New York Press, 1991): 125.

22. Boyarin, *Intertextuality*, 77.
23. Joseph Dan, "Midrash and the Dawn of Kabbalah," in *Midrash and Literature*, 130.
24. *Midrash Ha-Zohar* 2 (114b).
25. A. Van der Heide, "PARDES: Methodological Reflections on the Theory of the Four Sages," *Journal of Jewish Studies* 34 (Autumn 1983): 148. It was probably introduced in Moses de Leon's *Sefer ha-Pardes,* which itself is no longer extant but was cited in *Ra'ya Mehemna* and in *Tiqqunei Zohar.*
26. Marc Bregman, "Introduction," in Howard Schwartz's *The Four Who Entered Paradise* (Northvale, N.J.: Jason Aronson Inc., 1995): xvi. See Bregman's excellent presentation of the various talmudic versions of the story and his concise summary of their possible meanings.
27. For a description of this midrash, see page 13.
28. This is an alternative version to "Rabbi Akiva ascended in peace and descended in peace."
29. Bregman, "Introduction," xvi.
30. Van der Heide, "PARDES," 150–53. Look not only at the work of Moses de Leon, but also outside the *Zohar,* in the writings of such scholars as Bachya ben Asher ibn Halawa, Isaac ibn Latif, and Joseph ibn Gikatila.
31. Scholem, "The Meaning of the Torah in Jewish Mysticism," 53f. The earliest mention of four distinct levels of the study of Torah is found in *Midrash Ne'elam to the Book of Ruth.* However, it should be noted that in certain works on Jewish exegesis, a system of three, not four, levels of meaning is prevalent. Generally, the three include the literal, the midrashic, and the philosophic. See, for example, Van de Heide's citation of the work of the exegete and philosopher, Joseph ibn Aqnin ("PARDES," 154) in this regard.
32. *Zohar* 3, 152a.
33. Fishbane, *The Garments of Torah,* 114–16.
34. B.T. *Shabbat* 63a.
35. B.T. *Kiddushin* 49a.
36. Fishbane, *The Garments of Torah,* 116.
37. Max Kadushin, *The Rabbinic Mind* (New York: Bloch Publishing Co., 1972): 103–4.
38. *Shir ha-Shirim Rabbah* 2:2:5.
39. Neusner, *History and Torah: Essays on Jewish Learning,* 26.
40. Fishbane, *The Garments of Torah,* 119.
41. *Shir ha-Shirim Rabbah* 2:2:1.
42. *Zohar* 1, 1a.
43. F. Lachower and I. Tishby, *The Wisdom of the Zohar,* vol. 1, trans. David Goldstein (London: Oxford University Press, 1989): 391, n. 34.
44. There are numerous ways in which Torah is symbolized by water.
45. *Zohar* 2, 114b.
46. Levi Isaac of Berdichev, *Imrei Zaddikim,* 10.

47. Handelman, *The Slayers of Moses,* 47–49.
48. James Kugel, "Two Introductions to Midrash," in *Midrash and Litera-ture,* 93.
49. See page 19.
50. Boyarin, *Intertextuality,* 15ff.
51. Fishbane, *The Garments of Torah,* 27.
52. Boyarin, *Intertextuality,* 21.
53. Ibid., 128.
54. P.T. *B'rakhot* 2a.
55. *Mekhilta d'Rabbi Ishmael, Massekhta d'Pisha, parashah* 5.
56. See page 29.
57. See, for example, Romans 3:20–31, 4:2–16, 9:30–33, and 10:4–12, and Galatians 2:16–21, and 3:6–25, among many. The rejection of the law in Paul's writings is especially true when it comes to ritual observances such as the Sabbath, festivals, circumcision, and forbidden foods.
58. See, in this regard, my article, "Judaism and Christianity: The Parting of the Ways," *Thought: A Review of Culture and Ideas* 67 (December 1992): 410–20.
59. Boyarin, *Intertextuality,* 19.
60. Eugene Mihaly, *A Song to Creation* (Cincinnati: Hebrew Union College Press, 1975): 17–20.
61. Ibid., 21.
62. Ibid., 19.

Chapter 5

1. *Sifrei Devarim, piska* 305.
2. M. *Avot* 3:2.
3. Holtz, *Finding Our Way,* 205.
4. *Avot d'Rabbi Natan,* A, chapter 3.
5. See page 3.
6. See, in this regard, Handelman, *The Slayers of Moses,* 233.
7. *Mishlei Rabbah* 7:7:2. The translation of this passage is taken from Holtz, *Finding Our Way,* 198–99.
8. M. *Avot* 2:8.
9. See page 96.
10. M. *Avot* 6:9.
11. The translation of the passage from *Pirkei Avot* 6:1 is based on Fishbane, *The Garments of Torah,* 77.
12. See page 3.
13. B.T. *Avodah Zarah* 3b.
14. An alternative text reading here is "I will teach in order to be an Elder," i.e., one teaches in order for his fame to spread so that he may gain a seat in the academy.
15. For "wisdom" meaning Torah see page 40.
16. Holtz, *Finding Our Way,* 98.
17. See another parallel passage in *Sifrei Devarim, piska* 41.
18. The text reads literally "his *sela,*" which is a coin worth two shekels.

19. *Sifrei Devarim, piska* 48.
20. *Sifrei Devarim, piska* 41.
21. Reuven Hammer, *Sifre: A Tannaitic Commentary on the Book of Deuteronomy* (New Haven: Yale University Press, 1986): 416, n.1 (*piska* 48).
22. M. *Avot* 5:22.
23. *Avot d'Rabbi Natan,*A, chapter 3.

Conclusion

1. Kirk Douglas, *Climbing the Mountain: My Search for Meaning* (New York: Simon & Schuster, 1997): 144.
2. Crites, "The Narrative Quality of Existence," 295.
3. Franz Rosenzweig, *On Jewish Learning,* ed. by N. N. Glatzer (New York: Schocken Books, 1955): 98.
4. B.T. *Shabbat* 31a.
5. B.T. *Tamid* 31b.
6. This rendition is also found in the Targum (the Aramaic translation) of Leviticus 19:18. It is clear that there is a substantive difference between the rabbinic rendition of the Leviticus verse, which is negative and was circulated as early as the third century B.C.E. (see Tobit 4:15 in this regard), and the Christian version, which is positive: "Do unto others as you would have them do unto you" (Matthew 7:12, for example). It certainly is the case that the forceful positive version of the Gospels can lead to greater hurt, since it sets up the individual as the determinant of what is best for his or her fellow human being, based on what that individual likes. However, some Christian apologetes have argued that the Christian version is superior, since it is truly universal, while the Leviticus verse, which speaks of "your neighbor"—in Hebrew *re'acha,* which in the context of Leviticus 19 means "your fellow Israelite"—is highly particularistic. They ignore, however, that in the same chapter of Leviticus, we are told: "The stranger that sojourns with you shall be unto you as the home born among you, and *you shall love him as yourself* (Leviticus 19:33–34). For a discussion of this controversy, see R. Travers Herford, *Talmud and Apocrypha* (New York: Ktav Publishing House, Inc., 1971): 144–50.
7. *Sifra debei Rav* 89a. See also P.T. *Nedarim* 41c and *B'reishit Rabbah* 24:7.
8. See, in this regard, *Sifra* 109c.
9. *Mekhilta d'Rabbi Ishmael, Massekhta d'Va-Yassa, parashah* 1.
10. In this *Mekhilta* passage, the Rabbis suggest several possibilities, including the root of a fig tree and the root of a pomegranate.
11. Ibid.
12. For example, see the Song of Songs 4:8 and the rabbinic interpretation of it.

Glossary

Sometimes two pronunciations of words are common. This glossary reflects the way that many Jews actually use these words, not just the technically correct version. When two pronunciations are listed, the first is the way the word is sounded in proper Hebrew, and the second is the way it is sometimes heard in common speech, often under the influence of Yiddish, the folk language of the Jews of northern and eastern Europe. "Kh" is used to represent a guttural sound, similar to the German "ch" (as in "sprach").

amora (ah-moh-RAH or, commonly, ah-MOH-rah); pl. *amoraim* (ah-moh-rah-EEM): A title for talmudic authorities and, therefore, living roughly from the third to the fifth centuries. They were the successors of the *tannaim*.

Ashkenazi (ahsh-k'-nah-ZEE or, commonly, ahsh-k'-NAH-zee): From the Hebrew word *Ashkenaz*, meaning geographic area of northern and eastern Europe; *Ashkenazi* is the adjective, describing the liturgical rituals and customs practiced there, opposed to Sefardi, meaning the liturgical rituals and customs that are derived from Sefarad, Spain.

Avot (ah-VOHT): Literally "fathers" or "ancestors," this tractate of the **Mishnah** contains mainly wisdom and the moral teachings of the scholars whose legal opinions make up the remainder of the Mishnah.

Babylonian Talmud: See **Talmud**.

baraita (bah-RAHY-tah): Tannaitic material that is not included in the **Mishnah**. It literally means "that which is outside [the corpus of the Mishnah]."

bet midrash (bayt meed-RAHSH): "House of study"; a term for **synagogue**.

B'reishit Rabbah (B'-ray-sheet rah-BAH): One of the most commonly referenced midrashic texts compiled in the fifth century C.E., in the land of Israel, its core is a verse-by-verse treatment of the Book of Genesis.

Chamisha Chumshei Torah (KHAH-mee-sha khoom-shay TOH-rah): The Hebrew equivalent of **Pentateuch**, literally meaning "The Five Fifth Parts of the Torah." The English names for the five books of the **Torah** are Genesis, Exodus, Leviticus, Numbers and Deuteronomy. They are based on the titles in the Latin Bible, which were drawn from the Greek translations of the Hebrew names *B'reishit* (In the Beginning), *Shemot* (Names), *Vayikra* (And [God] Called), *Bamidbar* (In the Desert), and *Devarim* (Words or Commandments).

chavrutah (khah-vroo-TAH): One's **Torah** study partner.

Chumash (khoo-MAHSH): The first part of the Bible, which is read in the **synagogue** on Mondays, Thursdays, the Sabbaths and holidays. Also called "the five books of Moses" or the **Torah,** it contains the books *B'reishit* (In the Beginning), *Shemot* (Names), *Vayikra* (And [God] Called), *Bamidbar* (In the Desert), and *Devarim* (Words or Commandments). These names are the first key words mentioned in each book, but they also allude to the content of each one. The English names for the five books of the Torah—Genesis, Exodus, Leviticus, Numbers, and Deuteronomy—are based on the titles in the Latin Bible, which were drawn from the Greek translations of the Hebrew names.

daf yomi (dahf-yoh-MI): The tradition of studying a page of the Babylonian **Talmud** daily, resulting in the Talmud reading being completed and begun again every seven years.

darash (dah-RAHSH): "To seek, search or demand" [meaning from the biblical text]; the term "midrash" is derived from this Hebrew word.

davar aher (dah-vahr-AHKHER): "Another interpretation," of the Bible. The Bible text's openness to different meanings led traditional rabbinic leaders(and continues to lead today's(to create an unending number of interpretations, and the same individual may offer several of them.

d'Oraita (d'OH-rahy-tah): "From the Torah," used as a description of biblical ordinance. "From the Torah" carries more authority than *d'Rabbanan,* "of the Rabbis."

d'Rabbanan (d'RAH-bah-nan): "Of the Rabbis," used as a description of a rabbinic ordinance.

Ecclesiastes (Mishlei) Rabbah: A relatively late compilation in the **Midrash Rabbah,** compiled as late as the tenth century, that contains a mixture of midrashic styles and genres.

eits chayim (ayts khah-YEEM), pl. *atsei chayim* (ah-TSAY khah-YEEM): "The Tree of Life," the **Torah.**

Haftarah (hahf-tah-RAH or, commonly, hahf-TOH-rah): The section of Scripture taken from the prophets and read publicly as part of Shabbat and holiday worship services. From a word meaning "to conclude," since it is the "concluding reading," that is, it follows a reading from the **Torah.**

halakhah (hah-lah-KHAH or, commonly, hah-LAH-khah): The Hebrew word for "Jewish law." Used as an anglicized adjective, *halakhic* (hah-LAH-khic), meaning "legal." From the Hebrew word meaning "to walk, to go," so denoting the way on which a person should walk through life.

hakham (KHAH-kham): A wise person.

Ha-Sefarim (Hah-sephah-REEM): "The Books," used by the early Rabbis to refer to scripture.

Hasidic (khah-SIH-dihk): Of the doctrine generally traced to an eighteenth-century Polish Jewish mystic and spiritual leader known as Ba'al Shem Tov (called also the BeSHT, an acronym composed of the initials of his name). Followers are called *Hasidim* (khah-see-DEEM or khah-SIH-dim); sing., *Hasid* (khah-SEED or, commonly, KHA-sid) from the Hebrew word *chesed* (KHEH-sed), meaning "loving-kindness" or "piety."

hyponoia: "Deep sense of the text," a term used by Hellenistic writers to describe the understanding that is achieved by using metaphors or allegories, while preserving the words of text, to interpret the Bible. It is referred to in the *remez* method of text interpretation.

intertextuality: The juxtaposing of verses from different places in the Bible that have very different intentions, in order to teach. This was typical technique used by the Rabbis to teach **Torah.**

Jerusalem Talmud: See **Talmud.**

Kabbalah (kah-bah-LAH or, commonly, kah-BAH-lah): A general term for Jewish mysticism, but used properly for a specific mystical doctrine that began in western Europe in the eleventh or twelfth centuries; it was recorded in the *Zohar* in the thirteenth century, and then was further elaborated, especially in the Land of Israel (in Safed), in the sixteenth century. From a Hebrew word meaning "to receive," or "to welcome," and secondarily, "tradition," implying the receiving of tradition.

Keri (keh-REE): The way a word in the **Torah** should be read despite its written form.

Keriat ha-Torah (keh-ree-AHT ha-toh-RAH): The reading of **Torah** in the **synagogue**, in an annual cycle of readings; each reading is called a *parashah* (pl. *parashiyyot*). The readings serve as ritual teaching and study.

Ketiv (keh-TEEV): The written form of a word in the **Torah.**

Ketuvim (keh-too-VEEM): "Writings," also known as Hagiographa; the third section of the Bible, focusing on liturgical poetry (Psalms, Lamentations), love poetry (Song of Songs), Wisdom Literature (Proverbs, Job, Ecclesiastes), and historical compilations (Ruth, Ezra, Nehemiah, and Chronicles, as well as the Book of Daniel, which is a combination of history and prophecy).

Kiddushin (kee-doo-SHEEN): The **Mishnah** tractate on marriage law.

Kinyan Torah (kihn-yahn TOH-rah): "The Acquisition of Torah," Chapter 6 of *Pirkei Avot* which is entirely devoted to a discussion about **Torah** study. Its opening stresses Torah study for its own sake and not as a means to an end.

Kitvei Ha-Kodesh (KEET-vay hah-KOH-desh): "Holy Writings," a term emphasizing the written nature of the biblical text, in contrast to the oral form in which the rabbinic tradition was thought to have been originally transmitted.

kotz (kohtz): Literally, "thorn"; a term used by the Rabbis to mean "every small element of Torah." Each *kotz* can be the basis on which an interpretation is created.

Ma'ariv (mah-ah-REEV or, commonly, MAH-ah-reev): From the Hebrew word *erev* (EH-rev), meaning "evening": one of two titles used for the evening worship service (also called *Arvit*).

mashal (mah-SHAHL): An analogy, usually drawn from real-life experiences, used in a rabbinic text to make an important point in the text's message.

mayim chayim (mah-YEEM khah-YEEM): "The water of life," a term used to describe the **Torah.**

Mekhilta (meh-KHEEL-tah): An exegetic **midrash**, proceding verse by verse through the Book of Exodus, offering a variety of interpretations of each verse. It was compiled sometime during the amoraic period (third to fifth centuries) in Palestine.

Menahot (MEH-nah-khot): A **Mishnah** tractate generally dealing with sacrificial laws.

meshalim (meh-shah-LEEM): Parables that appear frequently in **midrash** and in aggadic, non-legal parts of the **Talmud.**

midrash (meed-RAHSH or, commonly, MID-rahsh); pl. *midrashim*: From the Hebrew word *darash,* "to seek search, or demand" [meaning from the biblical text]; also, therefore, a literary genre focused upon the explication of the Bible. By extension, a body of rabbinic literature that offers classical interpretations of the Bible.

Midrash Shir ha-Shirim Rabbah: The volume of **Midrash Rabbah** that covers the Song of Songs.

mikra (MIH-krah): "Reading," a rabbinic term for the Bible that underscores both the public reading of scripture in Jewish liturgy and the fact that this written text could actually be read.

Minchah (meen-KHAH or, commonly, MIN-khah): Originally the name of a type of sacrifice, then the word for a sacrifice offered during the afternoon, and now the name for the afternoon **synagogue** service usually scheduled just before nightfall. *Minchah* means afternoon.

Mishnah (meesh-NAH or, commonly, MISH-nah): The first written summary of Jewish law, compiled in the Land of Israel about the year 200 C.E., and therefore our first overall written evidence for the state of Jewish prayer in the early centuries.

Midrash Rabbah: A work made up of ten different midrashic compilations, one on each of the five books of the **Chumash** and the "Five Scrolls": the Song of Songs, Ruth, Lamentations, Ecclesiastes, and Esther. These ten independent works were compiled at very different times, most probably between the fifth and thirteenth centuries, and in different locales, and they exhibit a variety of midrashic styles. Unlike the **Mishnah,** they are not a code organized by topic; instead, their material follows the organization of the different biblical books. The most well-known anthology of classic midrashic texts.

Misterin (mees-teh-REEM): "The secret knowledge," used as another term for *Torah she-Ba'al Peh* (Oral Torah).

mitzvah (meetz-VAH or, commonly, MITZ-vah); pl. *mitzvot* (meetz-VOHT): A Hebrew word used commonly to mean "good deed," but in the more technical sense, denoting any commandment from God, and therefore, by extension, what God wants us to do. Reciting the *Sh'ma* morning and evening, for instance, is a *mitzvah.*

Nevi'im (neh-vee-EEM): "Prophets," the second part of the Bible, was later subdivided into the "Former Prophets" and the Latter Prophets." The former are narrative-historical works: Joshua, Judges, Samuel, and Kings.

The latter are literary creations from the oratory of the Prophets: the many chaptered books of Isaiah, Jeremiah, and Ezekiel, and the twelve Minor Prophets Hosea, Joel, Amos, Obadiah, Jonah, Micah, Habbakuk, Zephaniah, Haggai, Zechariah, and Malachi.

Notain ha-Torah (NOH-tayn hah-TOH-rah): "Adonai is the Giver of the Torah."

Palestinian Talmud: See **Talmud**.

PaRDeS: An acronym for the different levels of meaning, or modes of interpretation, of the **Torah**: *Peshat* (literal), *Remez* (allegorical), *Derash* (midrashic), and *Sod* (mystical). The use of this pun on *pardes,* which literally means "citrus orchard," is traced back to Moses de Leon, the author of the *Zohar,* in the thirteenth century, and later teachers, though the modern period, have frequently used this acronym.

Pentateuch: The Greek word for "five-volumed book," referring to the Hebrew Bible after the five parts of the **Torah** were transcribed on separate scrolls. The Hebrew equivalent is *Chamisha Chumshei Torah.*

peshat (peh-SHAHT): The simple, straightforward meaning of a verse.

Pesikta d'Rav Kahana (peh-SEEK-tah d'rahv kah-HAH-nah): A homiletic **midrash** compiled of sermons that was put together in the late fifth to early sixth century in the Land of Israel, offering readings for the holidays and special Sabbaths.

Pesikta Rabbati (peh-SEEK-tah rah-BAH-tee): Compiled in the late sixth to early seventh century, this collection of literary sermons is geared not only to **Torah** portions read on special occasions but also to prophetic portions and the psalms recited.

petihtaot (**sing.** *petihta*) (peh-tikh-tah-OHT): Sermonic introductions that introduce **Torah** portions. They begin most often by quoting and interpreting verses from the Prophets and mainly the writings with no obvious connection to the **Torah** portion.

Pirkei Avot (peer-KAY ah-VOHT): "Chapter of the Fathers"; a tractate of the **Mishnah**.

Rav (RAHV): Rabbi, "teacher."

remez (REH-mez): Meaning "hint" or "allusion," a method of interpretation that preserves the surface meaning of the **Torah** text but adds significantly to it. With *remez,* the words of Torah are frequently transposed to another realm of discourse through being made into metaphor. Through metaphor or allegory, while preserving the words of the text, we learn what the text "is really talking about."

sakhar (seh-KHAHR): A word typically used for the reward we earn by observing the commandments, especially the study of **Torah**.

Sanhedrin: The **Mishnah** tractate dealing mainly with the court system and aggadic traditions.

Sefer Ha-Hokhmah (SAY-fer hah-khokh-MAH): A work written by Rabbi Eleazer ben Judah of Worms that lists seventy-three "Gates of Wisdom," representing seventy-three distinct methods of midrashic interpretation, and show how each functions. This work demonstrates how different methods can be used to interpret the same verse, thereby producing contradictory meanings.

Sefer Torah (SAY-fer TOH-rah); pl. *Sifrei Torah* (sif-RAY toh-RAH or, commonly, SIF-ray TOH-rah): Torah scroll.

sefirot (seh-fee-ROHT): Ten different emanations of God in the world, representing the various aspects of God, the Divine attributes and power, and each associated with a wide range of metaphors, from colors and key words to names of biblical characters.

Shacharit (shah-khah-REET or, commonly, SHAH-khah-reet): The morning worship service; from the Hebrew word *shachar* (SHAH-khar), meaning "morning."

Shalshelet ha-kabbalah (shahl-SHEH-let hah-kah-bah-LAH): The "Chain of Tradition" that extends back to Sinai and forward to the messianic age.

Shechinah (sh'-khee-NAH or, commonly, sh'-KHEE-nah): God's Divine Presence, considered to be the feminine aspect of the Divine.

Shir ha-Shirim (SHEER ha-shee-rif-ihm): One of the Five Scrolls which is read on Passover.

Sh'ma (sh'MAH): The central prayer in the first of the three main units in the worship service, the second being the *Amidah* and the third being the reading of Torah. The *Sh'ma* comprises three citations from the Bible. The larger unit in which it is embedded (called the *Sh'ma* and Its Blessings) contains also a formal call to prayer *(Bar'khu)* and a series of blessings on the theological themes that, together with the *Sh'ma*, constitute a liturgical creed of faith. *Sh'ma*, meaning "hear," is the first word of the first line of the first biblical citation, "Hear O Israel, Adonai is our God, Adonai is One," which is the paradigmatic statement of the Jewish faith, the Jews' absolute commitment to the presence of a single and unique God in time and space.

siddur (see-DOOR or, commonly, SIH-d'r); pl. *siddurim* (see-door-EEM): From the Hebrew word *seder*, meaning "order," and therefore, by extension, the name given to the "order of prayers," or prayer book.

Sifrei Devarim (SEEF-ray deh-vah-REEM): An exegetic **midrash**, this work analyzes the text of the Book of Deuteronomy verse by verse, compiled sometime during the third to fifth centuries in the Land of Israel.

sod (sohd): Meaning "mystery," a level of interpreting **Torah** which points to the Kabbalists' sense of the mystery of Divine speech and words. It symbolizes the ultimate and eternal dimension of the text; it assumes that the **Torah** text has an inexhaustible depth that in the end leads the reader to an encounter with God.

Sotah (SOH-tah): A tractate in the **Mishnah** dealing with laws concerning the suspected adultress mentioned in Numbers 5:11–31, who is required to drink water into which a particular Torah passage is dissolved. This water ritual is meant to prove the wife's innocence.

Talmid hakham (tahl-MEED KHAH-kham): "A student of one who is wise."

synagogue: From the Greek *synagoge* (sih-nah-GOH-gay), meaning "gathering." The synagogue is a place for gathering, study and prayer. Also known as *bet k'nesset*, meaning "house of gathering," *bet midrash*, meaning "house of study," and *bet t'fillah*, meaning "house of prayer."

Talmud (tahl-MOOD or, commonly, TAHL-m'd): The name given to each of the two great compendia of Jewish law and lore compiled over several centuries, and ever since, the literary core of rabbinic heritage. The *Talmud Yerushalmi* (y'roo-SHAL-mee), the "Jerusalem Talmud," is earlier, a product of the Land of Israel generally dated about 400 C.E. The better-known *Talmud Bavli* (BAHV-lee), or "Babylonian Talmud," took shape in Babylonia (present-day Iraq), and is traditionally dated about 550 C.E. When people say "the" Talmud without specifying which one they mean, they are referring to the Babylonian version. *Talmud* means "teaching."

talmud Torah (tahl-MOOD TOH-rah): The study of **Torah**.

TaNaKh: An acronym which is derived from the initial letters of the three divisions of the Hebrew Bible: **Torah**, *Nevi'im* (Prophets), and *Ketuvim* (Writings).

Tanna (TAH-nah); pl. *tannaim* (tah-nah-EEM or, commonly, tah-NAH-yim): "Teachers" or "transmitters." The Rabbis who lived between the destruction of the Temple and the compilation of the Mishnah (70 C.E.–200 C.E.). They transformed Judaism from a religion based on land and a sacrificial system to one based on learning and prayer.

Torah (TOH-rah): Literally, "teaching" or "direction." Normally, the first part of the Bible, also called the Five Books of Moses, or the *Chumash,* which is read in the synagogue on Monday, Thursday, Shabbat and holidays. Used also, by extension, to mean all Jewish sacred literature (the Written Torah, or *Torah she-Bikhtav*) and, all the commentaries and interpretations of the Written Torah (known as Oral Torah, *Torah she-Ba'al Peh*).

Torah she-Ba'al Peh (TOH-rah she-bah-ahl-PEH): "The Oral Torah," the commentaries, interpretations, legal writings, and legends that students and teachers have woven around the Written Torah *(Torah she-Bikhtav)* that were thought to have been transmitted out loud rather than in writing.

Torah she-Bikhtav (TOH-rah she-BIKH-tahv): "The Written Torah," also referred to as **Mikra** or **Kitvei Ha-Kodesh**.

Torah l'shma (TOH-rah l'shmah): The study of **Torah** for its own sake.

Torat Moshe (TOH-raht MOH-shay): "The Torah of Moses," the earliest name for the first part of the Bible.

Tosefta (toh-SEPH-tah): A tannaitic interpretation and extension of the **Mishnah**, compiled slightly after it.

Vayikra Rabbah (vah-YEEK-rah rah-BAH): A midrash made up of a series of sermons on the triennial cycle portions of the Book of Leviticus, compiled in the late fifth to early sixth century in the Land of Israel.

Zohar (ZOH-hahr): A shorthand title for *Sefer Hazohar* (SAY-fer hah-ZOH-hahr), literally, "The Book of Splendor," which is the primary compendium of mystical thought in Judaism; written mostly by Moses de Leon in Spain near the end of the thirteenth century, and ever since, the chief source for the study of **Kabbalah**.

Suggestions for Further Reading

Alter, Robert. *The Art of Biblical Narrative*. New York: Basic Books, 1981.

Bialik, Hayyim Nachman. *Halakha and Aggadah*. Trans. Leon Simon. London: Education Dept. of the Zionist Federation of Great Britain, 1917.

Boyarin, Daniel. *Intertextuality and the Reading of Midrash*. Bloomington: Indiana University Press, 1990.

Cohen, Norman J. *Self, Struggle & Change: Family Conflict Stories in Genesis and Their Healing Insights for Our Lives*. Woodstock, Vt.: Jewish Lights Publishing, 1996.

Elkins, Dov Peretz. *The Wisdom of Judaism: An Introduction to the Values of the Talmud*. Woodstock, Vt.: Jewish Lights Publishing, 2007.

Fishbane, Michael. *The Garments of Torah: Essays in Biblical Interpretation*. Bloomington: Indiana University Press, 1989.

Handelman, Susan. *The Slayers of Moses: The Emergence of Rabbinic Interpretation in Modern Literary Theory*. Albany: The State University of New York Press, 1982.

Hartman, Geoffrey, and Sanford Budick, eds. *Midrash and Literature*. New Haven: Yale University Press, 1986.

Holtz, Barry, ed. *Back to the Sources: Reading the Classic Rabbinic Texts*. New York: Summit Books, 1984.

———. *Finding Our Way: Jewish Texts and the Lives We Lead Today*. New York: Schocken Books, 1990.

Iser, Wolfgang. *The Act of Reading: A Theory of the Aesthetic Response*. Baltimore: Johns Hopkins University Press, 1979.

Neusner, Jacob. *Invitation to the Talmud*. New York: Harper and Row San Francisco, 1984.

Sarna, Nahum. "Bible, Canon," *Encyclopedia Judaica,* vol. 4.

Steinsaltz, Adin. *The Essential Talmud*. Trans. Chaya Galai. New York: Basic Books, 1976.

Sternberg, Meir. *The Poetics of Biblical Narrative*. Bloomington: Indiana University Press, 1987.

Strack, H, and G. Stemberger. *Introduction to the Talmud and Midrash*. Minneapolis, Minn.: Fortress Press, 1996.

Visotsky, Burton. *Reading the Book: Making the Bible a Timeless Text*. New York: Schocken Books, 1996.

Index

Torah study *con't.*
Beruriah and, 48–49; blessings before study, 5, 6; capacity for, 42; *chavrutah* method, 96; children and slaves exclusion, 32; community, importance of, 100–102; a crown greater than royalty, 11–12, 31–32; finding a teacher imperative, 40; interactive reading, 74–75; intertextuality, 52–54, 86–91; *l'shma,* for its own sake, 28, 102–106; and Jewish survival, 23–25; *kotz* (thorn, irritation), importance of, 62; learning together, importance of, 95–99; as a lifelong pursuit, 107–110; literalism, opposition to, 78–81; Maimonides view, 11–12; a mirror, 27; *mitzvah* of, 5; as nails well planted, 56; neglect of, and suffering, 18; never too late to begin, 33–35; new meaning, deriving, 21; obligation to, 20–21; observance *vs.* study, 29–30; as personal insight source, 25–26; practice *vs.* study, 29–30; Rabbinical view, 11–13; renewed interest in, 95; *shakla v'tarya* (give and take discussion), 61; Sinai, begun at, 19; Tarfon, position on, 29; teachers, importance of, 95–97; teacher-student relationship, 21–22; transformational nature of, 28; turning text over and over, 107–110; who should?, 32–33; women and, 32, 44–49; words, *Ketiv–Keray,* written *vs.* read, 12
Torah text: active reading of, 74–75; indeterminate nature of, 71–72; many faces of, 75–76; Massoretes vocalization pattern; multiple meanings, 77–78; *PaRDeS,* levels of inter-pretation, 78–86; reading as determining meaning, 74–75;

recontextualizing, 92–93; syntax, 72; terseness and meaning, 71–73
Torat Moshe, 8–10
Tosefta, 79
Tree of Life, 116
Tsimtsum (contracting), 99

V
Va-yehi, and misfortune connotation, 16
Vayikra Rabbah, 15, 16, 29, 39, 52

W
Wisdom, 39, 103, 105
The Wisdom of Ben Sira, 10
Women: Ben Azzai view on, 45–48; Beruriah and *talmud Torah,* 48–49; Rabbinical views of, 44–48; and Torah study, 32, 44–49
Work, defined, 58
Writings *(Ketuvim),* 8, 10
Written Torah. *See* Torah

Y
Yavneh, 33
Yohanan ben Zakkai, Rabbi, 33
Yoke of heaven, 32
Yose ben Kisma, Rabbi, 102
Yossi ben Hanina, Rabbi, 41, 43

Z
Zohar. See Mysticism

Printed in the USA
CPSIA information can be obtained
at www.ICGtesting.com
JSHW012035140824
68134JS00033B/3066